Sunset

More Low-Fat
RECIPES

By the Editors of Sunset Books and Sunset Magazine

Sunset Publishing Corporation ■ **Menlo Park, California**

Lowfat Chicken, Shiitake & Bok Choy Soup (recipe on page 21) gains bold flavor from pungent Ginger-Garlic Paste.

Lowfat Meals for Good Health

Around the country, more and more cooks are putting lowfat meals on the menu. Why? Less fat means better health, of course—but beyond that, lowfat dishes simply taste great. In this new book of lowfat recipes, we show you how truly satisfying lean dishes can be. From rich-tasting appetizers like Yogurt Cheese & Tomato Torta to marvelous main courses such as Grilled Leg of Lamb & Pears to a whole chapter of great desserts, our selections prove that "deprivation dieting" is an outdated notion. The only thing these recipes are missing is fat.

All our recipes have been developed to conform to the American Heart Association (AHA) requirements for fat intake; in each, fat provides less than 30% of the calories.

In addition to the recipes, we offer practical help in the handy appendix starting on page 96. Here you'll find a glossary of nutrition-related terms, information on interpreting package labels and making lowfat substitutions for familiar foods, and more.

For our recipes, we provide a nutritional analysis (see page 6) prepared by Hill Nutrition Associates, Inc., of Florida. We are grateful to Lynne Hill, R.D., for her advice and expertise.

We thank Rebecca LaBrum for editing the manuscript. We also thank Beaver Brothers Antiques, Biordi Art Imports, Fillamento, and RH for accessories used in our photographs.

Research & Text
Sue Brownlee

Contributing Editor & Food Stylist
Cynthia Scheer

Special Consultant
Patricia Kearney, R. D.,
Clinical Dietitian,
Stanford University Hospital,
Stanford, California

Coordinating Editor
Linda J. Selden

Design
Joe di Chiarro

Illustrations
Dick Cole

Photography
Peter Christiansen: 2; **Tom Wyatt:** 7, 10, 15, 18, 23, 26, 31, 34, 39, 42, 47, 50, 55, 58, 63, 66, 71, 74, 79, 82, 87, 90, 95.

Photo Styling
Susan Massey

Cover: For a colorful and appealing dinner, offer quick-cooking Shrimp with Black Bean Sauce (recipe on page 54). Served on a crisp bed of shredded napa cabbage, the saucy shellfish are delicious with crusty Rosemary & Lemon Stretch Breadsticks (recipe on page 78), minted iced tea, and fresh fruits. Design by Susan Bryant. Photography by Tom Wyatt. Photo styling by Susan Massey. Food styling by Cynthia Scheer.

All of the recipes in this book were tested and developed in the Sunset test kitchens.

Senior Editor (Food and Entertaining), Sunset Magazine
Jerry Anne Di Vecchio

Editor, Sunset Books: Elizabeth L. Hogan

First printing January 1993

Copyright © 1993, Sunset Publishing Corporation, Menlo Park, CA 94025. First edition. World rights reserved. No part of this publication may be reproduced by any mechanical, photographic, or electronic process, or in the form of a phonographic recording, nor may it be stored in a retrieval system, transmitted, or otherwise copied for public or private use without prior written permission from the publisher. Library of Congress Catalog Card Number: 92-61758. ISBN 0-376-02480-1. Lithographed in the United States.

Contents

Special Features

■

Cooking the Lowfat Way

Lowfat cooking makes news! Just pick up the paper, leaf

through a magazine, or turn on the television and you'll

learn of another reason to cut back on fats in your diet. The

best news of all, though, is that lowfat foods aren't just

healthful, but wonderfully delicious and satisfying: dewy

fruits and crisp vegetables, glistening fish and flavorful

poultry, juicy lean meats and hearty whole grains. What's

more, adjusting your culinary style for cooking the lowfat

way can be almost effortless—just follow our cooking tips

and the dozens of great recipes in the next 10 chapters.

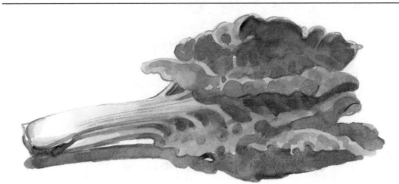

Learning about the Fats in Foods

Though the fats in foods are composed of three types of fatty acids—saturated, monounsaturated, and polyunsaturated—they're usually classified as just one of the three kinds, depending on which fat is present in greatest proportion.

Saturated fats, typically solid at room temperature, may raise your blood cholesterol level and increase the risk of heart disease if consumed in excess. These fats are found, for the most part, in red meats and dairy products and in some vegetable fats (such as coconut, palm, and palm kernel oils); poultry, fish, and shellfish also contain saturated fat in lesser amounts. *Hydrogenated* vegetable oils (those such as margarine and vegetable shortening, which have been converted to solid or semisolid form by the addition of hydrogen) are higher in saturated fat than the unhydrogenated forms.

Monounsaturated fats occur mainly in olive, peanut, and canola (rapeseed) oils. *Polyunsaturated fats* can be found in safflower, sunflower, corn, soybean, and cottonseed oils and in some fish. It's a good idea to focus on unsaturated fats for cooking and use at the table, since many nutritionists believe that these fats can help lower blood cholesterol. Just be sure to keep your total daily fat within the recommended limits (see "Health Effects of Fats & Cholesterol," below).

What about Cholesterol?

Cholesterol and fat are not the same thing. Cholesterol is a fatlike substance your body uses to synthesize vitamins and hormones and to form nerve sheaths and cell membranes. It's present in all animal foods: meats, poultry, fish, milk and milk products, and egg yolks. Both the meat and skin of poultry and the lean and fat portions of red meats contain cholesterol. Plant foods, on the other hand, are all cholesterol-free.

There are two kinds of cholesterol. Some cholesterol, enough for the body's needs, is manufactured in the liver; dietary cholesterol comes from the foods we eat. Both types affect the blood cholesterol level.

Health Effects of Fats & Cholesterol

Too much dietary fat—especially saturated fat—increases the risk of heart disease; it also contributes to obesity and certain types of cancer. Excess cholesterol is also associated with heart problems: too much dietary cholesterol can result in elevated blood cholesterol, which is linked to heart disease.

The effect of diet on blood cholesterol varies from one individual to the next, but blood cholesterol levels do tend to increase among those whose diets are high in calories, saturated fat, and cholesterol. Of these three factors, dietary saturated fat influences blood cholesterol the most.

Some health authorities recommend that dietary cholesterol be limited to 300 milligrams or less per day. Calories from fat should account for no more than 30% of the day's total. It's also advised that calories from saturated fat make up no more than 10% of the daily total—about 24 grams of fat, if you're allowed 2,200 calories a day.

For each recipe in this book, you'll find nutritional information stating the milligrams of cholesterol and grams of total fat and saturated fat per serving; in all cases, the calories from fat amount to 30% or less of the total calories.

The chart beginning on page 107 notes the grams of total and saturated fat in a typical serving of many common foods.

Choosing a Balanced Diet

It's an old story but one that's still true—if you eat a variety of foods, you can get all the nutrients you need, yet still stay within your calorie limits to maintain a healthy weight.

For help in making good daily food choices and planning menus, review the Food Guide Pyramid discussed on pages 98 and 99. This new nutrition plan (which replaces the earlier Four Food Group scheme) focuses on cutting down fat. Another useful aid in selecting heart-healthy meals is the American Heart Association (AHA) Diet (pages 102 and 103). You'll find that this diet lists more specific food choices than does the pyramid and groups foods somewhat differently—but it, too, is aimed at promoting lowfat eating.

Is Fiber Important?

In recent years, we've heard a lot about the virtues of dietary fiber—and it's natural to wonder if these claims have merit. In fact, foods high in dietary fiber (plant material that passes undigested through the intestine) do offer some health benefits. A fiber-rich diet can help lower blood cholesterol, protect against certain cancers, prevent constipation, and improve the control of blood sugar in diabetics.

There are two kinds of dietary fiber: soluble and insoluble. Many foods contain both kinds, but one type usually prevails. *Soluble fiber* has been shown to lower blood cholesterol levels; good sources include oats, legumes, barley, apples, carrots, and citrus fruits. The *insoluble fiber* in wheat bran, whole wheat, other whole grains, fruits, and vegetables has no known effect on blood cholesterol.

Nutritionists generally recommend a daily consumption of 25 to 35 grams of total fiber, both soluble and insoluble. To achieve this goal, cut back on processed foods and emphasize complex carbohydrates: whole grains, breads, cereals, fresh fruits, vegetables, and legumes. The AHA recommends that 55% of the day's calories come from complex carbohydrates—and in fact, eating plenty of these foods can help you stick to a lowfat eating plan. Complex carbohydrates supply concentrated energy and give you a fuller feeling, all for a relatively modest 4 calories per gram and a bonus of necessary vitamins and minerals.

When you shop for packaged foods, read the labels carefully (see page 106) to make sure the emphasis is on less fat and cholesterol as well as more fiber. Dishes like our Minestrone with Chard (page 25) and Apple, Cinnamon & Raisin Mini-muffins (page 76) make delicious high-fiber contributions to an overall lowfat diet.

Exercise Pays

Increasing your physical activity improves stamina and helps you manage your weight. Regular exercise can also raise levels of HDL or "good cholesterol" (see "Lipoproteins," page 97), lower blood pressure, and build bone mass.

For help in beginning an exercise program, take a look at "Exercising for Fitness" (pages 104 and 105). As you'll learn, you don't have to start running marathons or climbing mountains to reap the rewards of exercise; you can increase your fitness simply by taking a brisk 30- to 60-minute walk each day.

Lowfat Meals away from Home

Restaurateurs have good news for health-conscious people who eat out often. More and more menus—even those offered at fast-food outlets—reflect today's lowfat concerns. You'll find numerous lean choices: grilled chicken and fish, leaner burgers, light salads, and more.

If you're not sure what you'll find at a particular restaurant, call ahead and ask about the menu. If the selections seem too heavy, find out if the kitchen will accommodate special requests: ask if

the chef will grill meat, poultry, or fish instead of frying it, or if rich sauces can be omitted or served on the side.

Working with the AHA, many restaurants now use a special menu symbol to point out heart-healthy dishes made with a minimum of saturated fat. You can support this practice by letting your waiter know how pleased you are to find such healthful choices.

Cutting Cooking Fat

It's easy to enjoy the benefits of a lowfat diet when you use this book. To spark your interest and enthusiasm, have a look at the menus on pages 8 and 9: you'll find suggestions for incorporating a variety of our recipes in tempting full meals that are rich in vegetables, fruits, whole grains, legumes, and lowfat meats, poultry, and seafood.

As you prepare our recipes, you'll become familiar with a number of lowfat cooking techniques: baking, broiling, grilling, poaching, steaming, and browning with little or any oil. For more information on fat-lowering cooking methods, see page 100; page 101 suggests some ingredient substitutions you can use to trim down your favorite dishes.

About Our Nutritional Data

For our recipes, we provide a nutritional analysis stating calorie count; percentage of calories from fat, carbohydrates, and protein; grams of total fat, saturated fat, carbohydrates, and protein; and milligrams of cholesterol and sodium. Generally, the analysis applies to a single serving, based on the number of servings given for each recipe and the amount of each ingredient. If a range is given for the number of servings and/or the amount of an ingredient, the analysis is based on an average of the figures given.

The nutritional analysis does not include optional ingredients or those for which no specific amount is stated. If an ingredient is listed with a substitution, the information was calculated using the first choice.

*Contrasting flavors and temperatures—tart with sweet, hot with cold—
lend appeal to Spiced Pork & Orange Salad (recipe on page 28). Complement
the refreshing main dish with chilled white wine and oven-warm
Honey Wheat Mini-loaves (recipe on page 77).*

Lowfat Menus for Family & Friends

Pictured on page 55
Flavors of the Pacific

This quick-to-prepare dinner for four, featuring hot cooked fish atop cold pasta and greens, is good in warm weather and on cool days, too. In summer, use Bartlett pears for the dessert; in winter, try Bosc or Anjou pears.

> Broiled Salmon & Asian-style Noodles (page 54)
> Crisp Japanese Rice Crackers
> Baked Pears with Ginger (page 84)
> Hot or Iced Tea

Pasta Tonight

Just right for a frosty evening, this menu offers a warming repast for four to six hungry diners. The main dish takes about 3 hours to cook, but it simmers unattended in the oven for most of that time. You can sip the soup while you wait for the spaghetti to boil.

> Spinach & Buttermilk Soup (page 25)
> Steak & Spaghetti (page 36)
> Mixed Lettuce Salad
> Warm Italian Bread
> Tangerines & Bananas
> Chianti or Mineral Water

Bountiful Buffet

This colorful collection of recipes makes a delightful Mexican-style potluck. The meal serves six to eight amply.

> Braised Chicken with Green Chile Sauce (page 48)
> Lean Refried Black Beans (page 72)
> Shrimp & Spinach Slaw (page 30)
> Tortilla Sticks (page 78) or Warm Corn Tortillas
> Dessert Nachos with Fruit Salsa (page 85)
> Beer, Soft Drinks & Coffee

Autumn Salad Supper

The focus is on cold foods in this hearty menu for six. It's a pleasant meal for a warm fall weekend—and it's easy to enjoy while you're watching a football game. Serve the chilled golden soup as a first course.

> Spiced Purée of Carrot Soup (page 24)
> Cold Sliced Roast Turkey Breast
> Viennese Potato Salad (page 33)
> Pickles & Crisp Vegetable Sticks
> Whole Wheat Orange Bars (page 92)
> Lemon Sherbet
> White Wine or Beer
> Coffee

Easygoing Patio Barbecue

Gather together a group of six friends on a summer afternoon or evening, then enjoy these distinctive dishes outdoors on the patio. You can grill the corn as well as the beef—or, if you like, take it easier and steam the ears, enclosed in plastic wrap, in the microwave oven.

> Grilled Beef Pocket Sandwiches (page 37)
> Corn on the Cob
> Green & Red Cabbage Slaw with Lowfat Dressing of Your Choice
> Berry Yogurt Cheese Pie (page 93)
> Soft Drinks, Milk, or Lemonade

Winter Soup Special

On a cold night, nothing is quite as comforting as a kettle of hot, hearty soup; this one's thick with meat and plenty of vegetables. The menu serves six to eight.

Salad of Greens, Red Onion & Citrus
Beef & Pumpkin Soup (page 20)
Crusty Rye Bread
Warm Gingerbread (page 93)
Beaujolais Nouveau or Milk
Spiced Tea

Dinner with an Italian Accent

The cold cauliflower dish that begins this dinner for six appears in our collection of side dishes, but it's a nice choice for a first course as well. For a pretty presentation, arrange small servings on individual plates; garnish each with a sprig of mint.

Cauliflower with Toasted Mustard Seeds (page 69)
Braised Veal Shanks (page 38)
Barley & Brown Rice Pilaf (page 73)
Steamed New Peas
Orange Cake (page 94)
Pinot Grigio or Sauvignon Blanc
Coffee

Speedy Stir-fry

The main dish in this menu for four cooks quickly—so quickly that you can wait to start stir-frying until the rice and carrots served alongside are almost done.

Pork Stir-fry with Apple (page 40)
Steamed Rice
Nutmeg-dusted Steamed Baby Carrots
Sesame Breadsticks
Fresh Pineapple Spears
Tea or Milk

Herb Garden Pleasures

Fresh herbs enhance the savory flavors of this festive dinner for four. Because the dessert can be made with frozen berries, you can present the entire menu just about any time of year.

Buttercups (page 17)
Veal Chops & Sage Dressing (page 37)
Mushroom Risotto
Steamed Broccoli
Blueberry Buttermilk Sherbet (page 91)
White Zinfandel or Mineral Water
Espresso

Pictured on pages 15 and 63

Mediterranean Vegetable Medley

Here's a colorful meal for six that's sure to satisfy vegetarian friends—or anyone who just loves vegetables. Snack on the tangy cheese torta, scooping it onto crudités and toasted French bread slices, while you wait for the potatoes and their eggplant-pepper topping to bake.

Yogurt Cheese & Tomato Torta (page 14)
Ratatouille-topped Baked Potatoes (page 62)
Small Green Beans
Corn Muffins
Amaretti, Nectarine & Blueberry Crumble (page 85)
Iced Tea or Mineral Water with Lemon

Help yourself to these party treats! Skewered, grilled
Miso-marinated Pork with Apple & Onion (recipe on page 12)
and colorful Barley Sushi Scoops (recipe on page 13) are as
lean and light as they are luscious.

Appetizers

Celebrate appetizers as healthful and low in fat as they are delectable! Lead off a dinner party—or set a festive buffet table—with one or more of these lean morsels. Our tempting hors d'oeuvre and first-course treats include both hot bites and chilled tidbits, and many can be prepared in advance. Try sizzling skewered shrimp, juicy chicken meatballs, savory vegetable spreads, or luscious pesto-striped yogurt cheese. Choose just one appetizer to introduce a delicious lowfat repast; or offer several of your favorites together for a light meal.

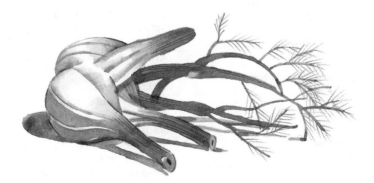

■ *Pictured on page 10*

Miso-marinated Pork with Apple & Onion

■

Per serving:
*165 **calories** (17% fat, 47% carbohydrates, 36% protein), 3 g **total fat** (1 g saturated), 19 g **carbohydrates**, 15 g **protein**, 42 mg **cholesterol**, 446 mg **sodium***

Preparation time: About 25 minutes

Marinating time: At least 1 hour

Grilling time: About 10 minutes

For a pretty beginning to a barbecue, offer skewered pork strips woven around wedges of apple and onion. *Aka miso* (red fermented soybean paste) is available in Asian markets.

- 1 **pound pork tenderloin, trimmed of fat**
- ⅓ **cup *each* aka miso and maple syrup**
- ¼ **cup sake, dry white wine, or water**
- 2 **tablespoons minced fresh ginger**
- 2 **medium-size apples such as McIntosh or Fuji (about 12 oz. *total*)**
  Lemon juice
- 1 **large onion, cut into wedges, layers separated**

Cut pork into ⅛-inch-thick, 6- to 7-inch-long slices; place in a 1-quart heavy-duty plastic bag. Add miso, syrup, sake, and ginger; mix well. Seal bag and refrigerate for at least 1 hour or until next day.

Core apples, cut into ½-inch wedges, and brush with lemon juice to prevent darkening. Lift pork slices from bag, reserving marinade in bag.

To assemble each skewer, thread tip of a thin metal skewer through end of a pork slice; thread on a piece of onion and an apple wedge, then thread skewer through pork again. Repeat process until skewer is full; you should have 8 skewers total.

Place skewers on a grill 4 to 6 inches above a solid bed of medium coals. Cook, basting with marinade and turning often, until meat is no longer pink in center; cut to test (about 10 minutes). Makes 8 servings.

Norwegian Meatballs

■

Per serving:
*81 **calories** (23% fat, 25% carbohydrates, 52% protein), 2 g **total fat** (1 g saturated), 5 g **carbohydrates**, 10 g **protein**, 22 mg **cholesterol**, 216 mg **sodium***

Preparation time: About 25 minutes

Cooking time: About 15 minutes

Use ground chicken breast to create an updated version of a long-time party favorite. Seasoned with sage and fennel, the delicate meatballs are served in a creamy cheese sauce.

- ¼ **cup low-sodium chicken broth or water**
- 6 **tablespoons all-purpose flour**
- 2 **pounds ground skinned chicken breast**
- 2 **large egg whites**
- 1 **teaspoon *each* dry sage and pepper**
- ½ **teaspoon *each* fennel seeds and salt**
  Gjetost Sauce (recipe follows)

In a bowl, smoothly mix broth and flour; then add chicken, egg whites, sage, pepper, fennel seeds, and salt. Mix well. Shape meat mixture into 1-tablespoon mounds (you will have about 48); set slightly apart in 2 nonstick or lightly oiled 10- by 15-inch baking pans.

Bake meatballs in a 500° oven for 10 minutes. Meanwhile, prepare Gjetost Sauce; keep hot. Turn meatballs over with a wide spatula and continue to bake until well browned on outside and no longer pink in center; cut to test (about 2 more minutes).

To serve, add meatballs to sauce; mix gently. Keep hot on a warming tray. Spear meatballs with small skewers to eat. Makes 24 servings.

Gjetost Sauce. In a wide frying pan, combine 1 large **onion,** chopped, with ¼ cup **low-sodium chicken broth.** Cook over high heat, stirring occasionally, until liquid evaporates and onion begins to brown. To deglaze, add ¼ cup more **low-sodium chicken broth** and stir to loosen browned bits. Cook, stirring occasionally, until liquid evaporates and onion begins to brown again. Stir in 2 tablespoons **cornstarch,** then smoothly mix in 2 more cups **low-sodium chicken broth.** Bring to a rapid boil over high heat, stirring. Reduce heat to low and add 1 cup (about 4 oz.) shredded **gjetost cheese;** stir until cheese is melted. Pour into a serving bowl; use hot (sauce thins if reheated).

Skewered Shrimp Packages

Per serving:
34 *calories* (11% fat, 30% carbohydrates, 59% protein), 0.4 g *total fat* (0.1 g saturated), 3 g *carbohydrates*, 5 g *protein*, 34 mg *cholesterol*, 38 mg *sodium*

Preparation time: About 40 minutes

Marinating time: At least 1 hour

Grilling time: About 2 minutes

Adorned with green-onion sashes, our grilled marinated shrimp look as good as they taste. You can wrap up the shrimp in advance, then chill the packages until you're ready to barbecue them.

- 24 **large raw shrimp (31 to 35 per lb.), shelled and deveined**
- ¼ **cup dry sherry or rice vinegar**
- 1 **tablespoon minced fresh ginger**
- 24 **green onions, cut to 6 inches in length**

In a bowl, mix shrimp, sherry, and ginger. Cover and refrigerate for at least 1 hour or until next day.

Meanwhile, in a wide frying pan, bring 1 inch of water to a boil. Add onions and boil, uncovered, until limp (15 to 30 seconds). Lift out and immerse in ice water until cool; drain. (At this point, you may cover and refrigerate until next day.)

Thread a thin metal skewer lengthwise into each shrimp, piercing it almost—but not quite—all the way through. Lay an onion flat. Center a skewered shrimp across center of onion; tie onion around shrimp. (At this point, you may cover and refrigerate for up to 4 hours.)

Lay skewered shrimp on a grill above a solid bed of hot coals. Cook, turning several times, until shrimp are opaque in center; cut to test (about 2 minutes). Makes 12 servings.

Pictured on page 10

Barley Sushi Scoops

Per serving:
85 *calories* (4% fat, 75% carbohydrates, 21% protein), 0.4 g *total fat* (0.1 g saturated), 17 g *carbohydrates*, 5 g *protein*, 20 mg *cholesterol*, 40 mg *sodium*

Preparation time: About 20 minutes

Cooking time: About 30 minutes

Here's a do-it-yourself party appetizer that's sure to get everyone involved. Simply present a bowl of sushi-seasoned barley and a tray of crisp lettuce leaves, then let guests serve themselves.

- 2 **cups water**
- ¾ **cup pearl barley, rinsed and drained**
- 1 **large carrot (about 4 oz.), finely diced**
- ⅓ **cup seasoned rice vinegar (or ⅓ cup distilled white vinegar plus 2 tablespoons sugar)**
- 1 **medium-size cucumber (about 8 oz.), finely diced**
- ⅓ **cup sliced green onions**
- 2 **tablespoons drained pickled ginger, chopped**
- 4 **ounces small cooked shrimp**
  Fish sauce (*nuoc mam* or *nam pla*) or salt
- 1 **green onion**
- 40 **to 48 medium-size butter lettuce leaves (about 1½ lbs. *total*), rinsed and crisped**

In a 1½- to 2-quart pan, bring water to a boil. Add barley; reduce heat to low, cover, and simmer for 20 minutes. Sprinkle carrot over barley. Cover and continue to simmer until barley is tender to bite (about 10 more minutes).

Remove barley from heat; drain. Let cool, uncovered, in pan; then transfer to a medium-size bowl and mix in vinegar, cucumber, sliced onions, ginger, and shrimp. Season to taste with fish sauce and spoon into a serving bowl. Garnish with whole onion.

To eat, spoon barley mixture onto lettuce; wrap to enclose, then eat out of hand. Makes 10 to 12 servings.

■ Pictured on facing page

Yogurt Cheese & Tomato Torta

■

Per serving:
77 calories (8% fat, 59% carbohydrates, 33% protein), 1 g
total fat (0.3 g saturated), 11 g carbohydrates, 6 g protein,
1 mg cholesterol, 75 mg sodium

Preparation time: About 35 minutes

Chilling time: At least 13 hours

Bright colors and bold flavors combine in this irresistible appetizer. Pesto made from dried tomatoes is layered with soft, tangy yogurt cheese, then presented with crisp baguette slices or bite-size raw vegetables.

> **Yogurt Cheese (recipe follows)**
> **Tomato Pesto (recipe follows)**
> **Rosemary sprigs**
> **Toasted baguette slices or bite-size pieces of raw vegetables**

Prepare Yogurt Cheese and Tomato Pesto.

Smoothly line a tall, wide-mouth 2-cup container (such as a bowl, basket without finish or dye, or a clean new flowerpot) with muslin or a double layer of cheesecloth. Press a fourth of the Yogurt Cheese evenly into bottom of container. Evenly distribute a third of the Tomato Pesto over cheese. Repeat layers to use remaining cheese and pesto, finishing with cheese.

Fold edges of cloth over cheese. Press gently to compact. If using a basket or flowerpot, set in a rimmed pan to catch liquid. Cover airtight and refrigerate for at least 1 hour or up to 6 hours; occasionally pour off liquid as it accumulates.

Fold back cloth; invert torta onto a serving plate. Lift off cloth. Garnish with rosemary sprigs. To eat, spread torta on toast slices. Makes about 2 cups (about 8 servings).

Yogurt Cheese. Line a fine strainer with muslin or a double layer of cheesecloth. Set strainer over a deep bowl (bottom of strainer should sit at least 2 inches above bottom of bowl). Spoon 4 cups **plain nonfat yogurt** into cloth. Cover airtight and refrigerate until yogurt is firm (at least 12 hours) or for up to 2 days; occasionally pour off liquid that drains into bowl. Gently press cheese to remove excess liquid.

Tomato Pesto. Soak 1 cup (about 2¼ oz.) **dried tomatoes** in **boiling water** to cover until soft (about 10 minutes). Drain; squeeze out excess liquid. Whirl tomatoes in a food processor (or chop with a knife) until minced. Mix tomatoes with 2 tablespoons grated **Parmesan cheese,** 1 clove **garlic** (minced or pressed), and 1 teaspoon minced **fresh rosemary** or ½ teaspoon dry rosemary. Season to taste with **salt.**

Favas with Herbs

■

Per serving:
93 calories (24% fat, 59% carbohydrates, 17% protein), 3 g
total fat (0.3 g saturated), 14 g carbohydrates, 4 g protein,
0 mg cholesterol, 171 mg sodium

Preparation time: About 5 minutes

Company coming and no time to fuss? If you keep a few cans of beans and some good-quality olive oil and wine vinegar on hand, you can serve up a tempting tidbit in minutes.

> 2 **cans (about 27 oz.** *each***) fava beans, drained and rinsed; or 3 cans (about 15 oz.** *each***) butter beans, drained and rinsed**
> ⅓ **cup minced red onion**
> ¼ **cup coarsely chopped fresh oregano or 1½ tablespoons dry oregano**
> 2 **tablespoons olive oil**
> ¼ **cup red wine vinegar**
> **Salt and pepper**
> **Sliced crusty bread; or miniature pita bread rounds (***each* **about 3 inches in diameter)**

In a bowl, mix beans, onion, oregano, oil, and vinegar. Season to taste with salt and pepper. If made ahead cover and refrigerate for up to 1 day; serve at room temperature. To eat, spoon onto bread. Makes about 5 cups (about 12 servings).

To make this stylish *Yogurt Cheese & Tomato Torta (recipe on facing page)*, you layer tangy, easy-to-make yogurt cheese with a rosemary-scented pesto based on dried tomatoes. Spread the torta on toasted French bread and your choice of crisp raw vegetables.

Roasted Fennel & Carrots with Belgian Endive

Per serving:
46 *calories* (13% *fat*, 70% *carbohydrates*, 17% *protein*), 1 g *total fat* (0.1 g saturated), 8 g *carbohydrates*, 2 g *protein*, 0 mg *cholesterol*, 69 mg *sodium*

Preparation time: About 35 minutes

Cooking time: About 50 minutes

When cool days call for rich flavors, start off a casual company supper with this hearty dip. For entertaining ease, you can prepare it up to 3 days in advance. (To ensure proper seasoning, make the dip only with unsalted homemade or canned low-sodium broth.)

- 2 medium-size heads fennel (about 1 lb. *each*)
- 5 cups finely chopped carrots (about 2 lbs.)
- 2 large onions, finely chopped
- 2 teaspoons *each* cumin seeds and mustard seeds
- 4 cloves garlic, minced or pressed
- 5¼ cups unsalted chicken broth or 3 cans (about 14½ oz. *each*) low-sodium chicken broth
  Salt and pepper
- 6 heads Belgian endive (about 1 lb. *total*), separated into leaves, rinsed, and crisped

Cut feathery tops from fennel; wrap in a damp paper towel, enclose in a plastic bag, and refrigerate until ready to use (or for up to 3 days).

Cut root ends and any bruised spots from fennel heads, then finely chop fennel and place in a 5- to 6-quart pan. Add carrots, onions, cumin seeds, mustard seeds, garlic, and ½ cup of the broth. Cook over high heat, stirring occasionally, until liquid evaporates and vegetables begin to brown. To deglaze, add ¼ cup more broth and stir to loosen browned bits. Cook, stirring occasionally, until liquid evaporates and vegetables begin to brown again. Repeat deglazing step, using ¼ cup more broth each time, until vegetables are richly browned and all broth has been used (about 50 minutes *total*).

Season vegetable dip to taste with salt and pepper; serve warm or at room temperature. If made ahead, cover and refrigerate for up to 3 days; bring to room temperature before serving.

To serve, mound dip in a serving bowl, garnish with fennel tops, and set on a platter. Arrange endive leaves on platter around dip; spoon dip into leaves to serve. Makes about 4 cups (about 20 servings).

Falafel Pizza

Per serving:
75 *calories* (20% *fat*, 57% *carbohydrates*, 23% *protein*), 2 g *total fat* (0.2 g saturated), 11 g *carbohydrates*, 4 g *protein*, 21 mg *cholesterol*, 152 mg *sodium*

Preparation time: About 20 minutes

Baking time: About 35 minutes

A prebaked cheese crust forms the savory base for this unusual pizza. Garnished with green onion curls, the handsome pie is topped with green chiles and falafel in place of the usual tomato sauce and mozzarella. Serve it in thin wedges, with yogurt for dipping.

- 3 large eggs
- ¾ cup nonfat milk
- 1 small can (about 4 oz.) diced green chiles
- 1 package (6 to 8 oz.) falafel mix
- 1 about 12-inch-diameter Italian bread shell (about 1 lb.)
  Thinly sliced green onion
- 1 to 1½ cups plain nonfat yogurt

In a large bowl, beat eggs, milk, chiles, and falafel mix to blend well. Cover and let stand until falafel mix has absorbed moisture (about 10 minutes).

Place bread shell, cup side up, on a 14- by 17-inch baking sheet. Scrape falafel mixture into center of shell and spread smoothly to fill hollow. Bake in a 350° oven until center feels firm when lightly pressed (about 35 minutes). Garnish with onion.

Serve pizza warm or at room temperature. To serve, cut into thin wedges (about ¾ inch wide at rim); eat out of hand. Offer yogurt for dipping. Makes about 32 wedges (about 32 servings).

Lowfat Beverages

It's easy to add lowfat beverages to your repertoire: simply focus on fruits, vegetables, juices, sparkling water, and lowfat dairy products. To get you started, here are three choices—one warmly comforting, two cool and refreshing.

Hot Rum Eggnog

Preparation time: About 10 minutes
Cooking time: About 5 minutes

- 2 cups nonfat milk
- 1 tablespoon cornstarch
  About ¼ teaspoon freshly grated nutmeg
- 2 large egg whites
- ¼ cup sugar
- ¼ cup rum

In a 1- to 1½-quart pan, smoothly blend milk with cornstarch and ⅛ teaspoon of the nutmeg. Set aside.

In a large bowl, beat egg whites with an electric mixer until foamy. With mixer on high speed, gradually add sugar, beating until whites hold short peaks.

Stir milk mixture over high heat just until boiling. With mixer on medium speed, immediately pour hot milk mixture into beaten egg whites (don't pour directly onto beaters), scraping down bowl sides. Let stand for at least 4 minutes.

Add rum to eggnog, then pour eggnog through a fine strainer into small mugs. Dust with remaining nutmeg. Makes about 4½ cups (about 9 servings).

Per serving: 62 calories (2% fat, 76% carbohydrates, 22% protein), 0.1 g total fat (0.1 g saturated), 9 g carbohydrates, 3 g protein, 1 mg cholesterol, 41 mg sodium

Strawberry Shrub

Preparation time: About 5 minutes

- 1 cup hulled strawberries
- 1 cup orange juice
- 1 tablespoon balsamic vinegar
- ½ cup small ice cubes or crushed ice
- 1 to 3 teaspoons sugar
- 2 cups chilled sparkling water

Reserve 2 of the prettiest strawberries. Place remaining berries in a blender; add orange juice, vinegar, and ice cubes. Whirl until smooth; sweeten to taste with sugar.

Pour into 4 tall glasses, filling each about halfway; then pour ½ cup of the sparkling water into each glass. To garnish, cut reserved berries into halves; slash each berry half partway through and slip onto rim of a glass. Makes about 4 cups (4 servings).

Per serving: 48 calories (3% fat, 92% carbohydrates, 5% protein), 0.2 g total fat (0 g saturated), 12 g carbohydrates, 1 g protein, 0 mg cholesterol, 1 mg sodium

Buttercups

Preparation time: About 20 minutes
Broiling time: About 10 minutes

- 2 large yellow or orange bell peppers (about 1 lb. *total*), cut into halves lengthwise
- 2 cups small ice cubes or crushed ice
- 1 cup buttermilk
- 2 tablespoons lemon juice
- ½ teaspoon cumin seeds
  Salt
- 1 tablespoon minced fresh dill or 1 teaspoon dry dill weed
- 4 green onions

Place bell pepper halves, cut sides down, in a foil-lined 10- by 15-inch baking pan. Broil peppers about 4 inches below heat until charred (about 10 minutes). Remove from oven, cover with foil, and let cool.

Pull off and discard skins, stems, and seeds from peppers. Drain liquid from baking pan into a blender; add peppers, ice cubes, buttermilk, and lemon juice. Whirl until smoothly puréed. Stir in cumin seeds; season to taste with salt. Pour into 4 tall glasses and sprinkle with dill; add an onion as a stirrer to each glass. Makes about 3⅔ cups (4 servings).

Per serving: 57 calories (11% fat, 69% carbohydrates, 20% protein), 1 g total fat (0.4 g saturated), 11 g carbohydrates, 3 g protein, 2 mg cholesterol, 71 mg sodium

*Tender pasta bow ties and fresh zucchini slices mingle in savory
Italian Sausage Soup (recipe on page 20), a hearty choice for a family supper.
You make the simple Italian sausage yourself by mixing minced lean
pork with wine, herbs, and garlic.*

Soups

Soups spell satisfaction, especially for cooks in search of tempting lowfat dining choices. Thick, fragrant, and hearty, our nutritious soups are nonetheless surprisingly lean. For a richly flavored first course, try tangy Spinach & Buttermilk Soup or a velvety, curry-seasoned carrot soup drizzled with watercress purée. Or savor a robust main-dish choice such as make-ahead Italian Sausage Soup or zesty Salsa Fish Soup. Whatever your selection, you'll be delighted by the ease of preparation and fresh, natural flavors.

Beef & Pumpkin Soup

Per serving:
181 *calories* (28% fat, 43% carbohydrates, 29% protein), 6 g
total fat (1 g saturated), 21 g **carbohydrates**, 14 g **protein**,
19 mg **cholesterol**, 128 mg **sodium**

Preparation time: About 25 minutes

Cooking time: About 55 minutes

Coarsely mashed Hubbard or banana squash—
called "pumpkin" by the islanders of St. Lucia—
adds texture to this homespun Caribbean soup.

- 1 **tablespoon salad oil**
- 1 **large onion, chopped**
- 1 **stalk celery, thinly sliced**
- 8 **cups low-sodium chicken broth**
- 8 **ounces lean boneless beef chuck, trimmed of fat and cut into ½-inch cubes**
- 3½ **pounds Hubbard or banana squash, peeled, seeded, and cut into ½-inch cubes (you should have about 10 cups)**
- 2 **large carrots (about 8 oz. *total*), coarsely chopped**
- 8 **ounces spinach**
  Salt and pepper

Heat oil in a 6- to 8-quart pan over medium-high
heat. Add onion and celery; cook, stirring often,
until onion is soft (about 7 minutes). Add broth
and beef. Bring to a boil; then reduce heat, cover,
and simmer for 30 minutes. Add squash and
carrots. Bring to a boil; then reduce heat, cover,
and simmer until squash and beef are very tender
when pierced (about 15 more minutes).

Meanwhile, discard tough stems and any
yellow or wilted leaves from spinach. Rinse well,
drain, and cut crosswise into ¼-inch-wide strips.

With a slotted spoon, lift about three-fourths of
the squash from pan; mash coarsely. Return mashed
squash to pan along with spinach. Bring to a boil
over high heat; then reduce heat and simmer, uncovered, until spinach is wilted (about 3 minutes).
Skim and discard fat from soup; season soup to taste
with salt and pepper. Makes 6 to 8 servings.

Pictured on page 18

Italian Sausage Soup

Per serving:
306 *calories* (12% fat, 53% carbohydrates, 35% protein), 4 g
total fat (1 g saturated), 36 g **carbohydrates**, 24 g **protein**,
49 mg **cholesterol**, 952 mg **sodium**

Preparation time: About 20 minutes

Cooking time: About 40 minutes

Homemade sausage based on lean pork tenderloin
starts this lowfat soup off right. Packed with
vegetables and pasta, it's a hearty main course you
can prepare a day ahead, then reheat.

- **No-fat Italian Sausage (recipe on facing page)**
- 2 **large onions, chopped**
- 2 **cloves garlic, minced or pressed**
- 5 **cups beef broth**
- 1 **large can (about 28 oz.) pear-shaped tomatoes**
- 1½ **cups dry red wine**
- 1 **tablespoon *each* dry basil and sugar**
- 1 **medium-size green bell pepper (about 6 oz.), seeded and chopped**
- 2 **medium-size zucchini (about 8 oz. *total*), cut into ¼-inch-thick slices**
- 2 **cups (about 5 oz.) dry pasta bow ties (about 1½-inch size)**
- ½ **cup chopped parsley**
  Salt and pepper

Prepare No-fat Italian Sausage; refrigerate.

In a 5- to 6-quart pan (preferably nonstick),
combine onions, garlic, and 1 cup of the broth.
Bring to a boil over high heat; boil, uncovered,
stirring occasionally, until liquid evaporates and
vegetables start to brown (about 10 minutes). To
deglaze, add 3 tablespoons water and stir to loosen
browned bits. Cook, stirring occasionally, until liquid
evaporates and mixture begins to brown again
(about 1 minute). Repeat deglazing step about 3
more times, or until mixture is richly browned.

Stir in sausage and ½ cup more water. Cook,
stirring gently, until liquid evaporates and meat
begins to brown (about 8 minutes).

Add remaining 4 cups broth. Stir to loosen
browned bits. Cut up tomatoes; then add tomatoes

and their liquid, wine, basil, sugar, bell pepper, zucchini, and pasta to pan. Bring to a boil over high heat. Reduce heat, cover, and simmer until pasta is just tender to bite (about 15 minutes). If made ahead, let cool, then cover and refrigerate until next day.

Serve soup hot; sprinkle with parsley and season to taste with salt and pepper. Makes 6 servings.

No-fat Italian Sausage. Cut 1 pound **pork tenderloin** or boned pork loin, trimmed of fat, into 1-inch chunks. Whirl in a food processor, about half at a time, until coarsely chopped (or put through a food chopper fitted with a medium blade). In a bowl, mix pork, ¼ cup **dry white wine,** 2 tablespoons chopped **parsley,** 1½ teaspoons crushed **fennel seeds,** ½ teaspoon **crushed red pepper flakes,** and 2 cloves **garlic,** minced. If made ahead, cover airtight and refrigerate until next day.

■ *Pictured on page 2*

Chicken, Shiitake & Bok Choy Soup

■

Per serving:
471 calories (18% fat, 42% carbohydrates, 40% protein), 9 g total fat (2 g saturated), 49 g carbohydrates, 47 g protein, 99 mg cholesterol, 230 mg sodium

Preparation time: About 25 minutes

Cooking time: About 35 minutes

Too pretty to eat? Almost, but this combination of tender-crisp vegetables, rice, and chicken in a clear broth is too tempting to resist. A bold ginger-garlic paste gives each bowlful a flavor boost.

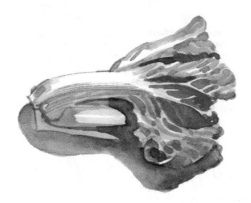

Ginger-Garlic Paste (recipe follows)
- 1½ **tablespoons Oriental sesame oil or salad oil**
- ⅓ **pound fresh shiitake or regular mushrooms, thinly sliced**
- 8 **green onions, sliced**
- 3 **cups low-sodium chicken broth**
- 4 **skinned, boned chicken breast halves (about 6 oz. *each*)**
- 2 **large carrots (about 8 oz. *total*), cut into thin slanting slices**
- 8 **baby bok choy (about 12 oz. *total*), coarse outer leaves removed**
- 2 **cups hot cooked short- or medium-grain rice**
- 3 **tablespoons minced cilantro**

Prepare Ginger-Garlic Paste and set aside.

Heat oil in a 4- to 5-quart pan over medium heat. Add mushrooms and half the onions; cook, stirring often, until mushrooms are lightly browned (about 10 minutes). Add broth and stir to loosen browned bits. Cover pan and bring broth to a boil over high heat.

Rinse chicken; pat dry. Add chicken and carrots to boiling broth, making sure they are covered with liquid. Reduce heat to low, cover pan tightly, and simmer until chicken is no longer pink in thickest part; cut to test (about 15 minutes).

Lift chicken to a cutting board. Add bok choy and remaining onions to pan; cover and simmer over medium heat until bok choy is bright green and just tender when pierced (about 5 minutes). Meanwhile, cut chicken across the grain into ½-inch-wide slanting slices.

Place a ½-cup scoop of rice off center in each of 4 wide, shallow soup bowls. Arrange a sliced chicken breast around each mound of rice. With a slotted spoon, distribute vegetables evenly among bowls. Stir cilantro into broth; gently pour into bowls over chicken and vegetables. Season each serving with about 2 tablespoons Ginger-Garlic Paste. Makes 4 servings.

Ginger-Garlic Paste. In a blender or food processor, combine ¾ cup coarsely chopped **fresh ginger,** 3 cloves **garlic,** and 3 tablespoons **seasoned rice vinegar** (or 3 tablespoons distilled white vinegar plus 1 tablespoon sugar). Whirl until very smooth. If made ahead, cover and refrigerate for up to 4 hours.

Pictured on facing page

Salsa Fish Soup

Per serving:
354 calories (12% fat, 55% carbohydrates, 33% protein), 5 g total fat (1 g saturated), 48 g carbohydrates, 29 g protein, 40 mg cholesterol, 512 mg sodium

Preparation time: About 5 minutes

Cooking time: About 20 minutes

When you want dinner *fast*, try this easy meal-in-a-bowl. The results are delicious, cleanup is minimal, and you can be out of the kitchen in under half an hour—or in less than 15 minutes, if you use quick-cooking rice.

- 6 cups low-sodium chicken broth
- ⅔ cup regular or quick-cooking rice
- 2 cups frozen corn kernels
- 1 pound skinned, boned mild-flavored white-fleshed fish (such as rockfish or lingcod), cut into 1-inch chunks
- 1 cup refrigerated or canned tomato-based chunk-style salsa; or 1 cup canned Mexican-style stewed tomatoes
  Lime wedges

In a 5- to 6-quart pan, combine broth and rice. Bring to a boil over high heat. Reduce heat, cover, and simmer until rice is tender to bite (about 15 minutes; about 5 minutes for quick-cooking rice). Add corn, fish, and salsa. Cover and simmer until fish is just opaque in thickest part; cut to test (about 5 minutes). Offer lime wedges to squeeze into soup to taste. Makes 4 servings.

Shrimp & Cannellini Soup

Per serving:
303 calories (20% fat, 50% carbohydrates, 30% protein), 7 g total fat (1 g saturated), 38 g carbohydrates, 23 g protein, 73 mg cholesterol, 610 mg sodium

Preparation time: About 15 minutes

Cooking time: About 30 minutes

No one needs to know that this elegant purée is made with canned beans! The pretty garnish of tiny pink shrimp and the appealing flavor will attract all the attention.

- 1 tablespoon salad oil
- 2 large onions, chopped
- 1 cup thinly sliced celery
- 3 cloves garlic, minced or pressed
- 2 cans (about 15 oz. *each*) cannellini beans, drained and rinsed
- 4 cups low-sodium chicken broth
- ¼ cup catsup
- 2 tablespoons dry sherry (optional)
- ⅓ pound small cooked shrimp
- ¼ cup chopped parsley
  Salt and pepper

Heat oil in a 4- to 5-quart pan over medium-high heat. Add onions, celery, and garlic; cook, stirring often, until all vegetables are browned (about 20 minutes).

Transfer vegetable mixture to a food processor or blender; add half the beans and 2 cups of the broth. Whirl until smoothly puréed, then return to pan. Purée remaining beans with remaining 2 cups broth; add to pan. Stir in catsup and, if desired, sherry. (At this point, you may cover and refrigerate until next day.)

To serve, stir soup over medium heat until hot. Ladle soup into 4 bowls; top equally with shrimp and parsley. Season to taste with salt and pepper. Makes 4 servings.

In little more time than it takes to get out the soup bowls and warm some
corn tortillas, you can make tangy Salsa Fish Soup (recipe on facing page).
Choose your favorite mild-flavored fish; rock cod, lingcod, or rockfish such
as Atlantic ocean perch or Pacific red snapper all fill the bill nicely.

Black Bean Soup

Per serving:
*270 **calories** (17% fat, 61% carbohydrates, 22% protein), 5 g **total fat** (1 g saturated), 43 g **carbohydrates**, 15 g **protein**, 0 mg **cholesterol**, 865 mg **sodium***

Preparation time: About 10 minutes

Cooking time: About 30 minutes

Thick, flavorful, and simple to prepare, this hearty soup is delightful topped with cheese, sour cream, and baked tortilla chips. To get things off to an especially quick start, use instant refried black beans (sold in natural-foods stores).

- 2 **teaspoons salad oil**
- 1 **large onion, chopped**
- 1¾ **or 2¾ cups low-sodium chicken broth**
- 1 **large can (about 28 oz.) tomatoes**
- 3 **cans (about 15 oz. *each*) black beans, drained, rinsed, and puréed; or 1 package (about 7 oz.) instant refried black bean mix**
- 1 **fresh jalapeño chile, seeded and minced**
- 2 **teaspoons cumin seeds**
  Condiments (choices follow)

Heat oil in a 5- to 6-quart pan over medium heat. Add onion and cook, stirring often, until golden (about 20 minutes). Add 1¾ cups broth (2¾ cups if using refried bean mix). Cut up tomatoes; then add tomatoes and their liquid, beans, chile, and cumin seeds to pan. Bring to a boil over high heat; reduce heat and simmer, uncovered, until soup is thick and flavors are blended (about 7 minutes).

To serve, ladle soup into bowls; offer condiments to add to taste. Makes 4 servings.

Condiments. Offer shredded **reduced-fat Cheddar cheese, reduced-fat sour cream, cilantro sprigs, baked tortilla chips,** and **lime wedges.**

Spiced Purée of Carrot Soup

Per serving:
*196 **calories** (19% fat, 68% carbohydrates, 13% protein), 4 g **total fat** (1 g saturated), 34 g **carbohydrates**, 7 g **protein**, 0.2 mg **cholesterol**, 130 mg **sodium***

Preparation time: About 25 minutes

Cooking time: About 25 minutes

Chilling time: At least 7 hours

As an extra convenience to the cook, this curry-seasoned soup can be made a day in advance, ready to be served cold. A colorful watercress purée garnishes the flavorful blend of carrots, onion, and potatoes.

- 1 **tablespoon olive oil**
- 1½ **pounds carrots, thinly sliced**
- 1 **pound onions, chopped**
- 1 **cup chopped celery**
- 1 **pound russet potatoes, peeled and cut into ½-inch cubes**
- 1 **teaspoon *each* ground cumin and curry powder**
- 6 **cups low-sodium chicken broth**
- 3 **tablespoons lemon juice**
  Cress Purée (recipe follows)

Heat oil in a 4- to 5-quart pan over medium-high heat. Add carrots, onions, and celery. Cover and cook, stirring often, until vegetables begin to brown (about 12 minutes). Add potatoes, cumin, curry powder, and broth. Bring to a boil over high heat; then reduce heat, cover, and simmer until potatoes are tender when pierced (about 10 minutes). Stir in lemon juice.

In a blender or food processor, whirl soup, a portion at a time, until puréed. Let cool slightly, then cover and refrigerate until cold (at least 7 hours) or until next day.

To serve, prepare Cress Purée. Pour soup into 6 bowls; drizzle with Cress Purée. Makes 6 servings.

Cress Purée. In a blender, combine 1 cup lightly packed **watercress sprigs** and ¼ cup **plain nonfat yogurt.** Whirl until puréed.

Minestrone with Chard

Per serving:
200 **calories** *(16% fat, 62% carbohydrates, 22% protein), 4 g* **total fat** *(0.4 g saturated), 32 g* **carbohydrates,** *11 g* **protein,** *3 mg* **cholesterol,** *1,376 mg* **sodium**

Preparation time: About 35 minutes

Cooking time: About 30 minutes

Whether served hot for a cool-weather lunch or at room temperature for dinner on a warm summer evening, this vegetable-rich soup is sure to be a hit. Round out the meal with crunchy-crusted whole-grain bread and fresh fruit.

- 1 **tablespoon olive oil**
- 1 **large onion, chopped**
- 1 **clove garlic, minced or pressed**
- 2 **stalks celery, diced**
- 2 **ounces thinly sliced Canadian bacon, cut into thin shreds**
- 3 **quarts beef broth**
- 2 **large carrots (about 8 oz.** *total***), diced**
- 1 **tablespoon minced fresh rosemary or 1 teaspoon dry rosemary**
- ⅔ **cup medium-grain rice**
- 1 **pound Swiss chard**
- 3 **cans (about 15 oz.** *each***) pinto beans, drained and rinsed**
- 1 **large can (about 28 oz.) pear-shaped tomatoes, drained and chopped**
- 8 **ounces green beans, cut into 1-inch lengths**
- 1 **pound zucchini, cut into ¾-inch-thick slices**
  Freshly grated Parmesan cheese
  Salt and pepper

Heat oil in an 8- to 10-quart pan over medium-high heat. Add onion, garlic, celery, and bacon; cook, stirring often, until onion is soft (about 8 minutes). Add broth, carrots, rosemary, and rice. Bring to a boil over high heat; reduce heat, cover, and simmer for 10 minutes.

Meanwhile, discard discolored ends from chard; then rinse chard well, drain, and cut cross-wise into ¼-inch-wide strips. Set aside. Mash a third of the pinto beans. Add mashed and whole pinto beans, tomatoes, green beans, and zucchini to pan. Bring to a boil over high heat; reduce heat, cover, and simmer for 5 minutes. Stir in chard; simmer, uncovered, until zucchini is tender to bite (about 5 more minutes). If made ahead, let cool; then cover and refrigerate until next day.

Serve soup hot or at room temperature; offer cheese, salt, and pepper to season soup to taste. Makes 10 to 12 servings.

Spinach & Buttermilk Soup

Per serving:
114 **calories** *(22% fat, 49% carbohydrates, 29% protein), 3 g* **total fat** *(1 g saturated), 14 g* **carbohydrates,** *8 g* **protein,** *5 mg* **cholesterol,** *235 mg* **sodium**

Preparation time: About 10 minutes

Cooking time: About 10 minutes

Made with a minimum of time and ingredients, this creamy soup is a versatile treat. Try it as the first course of a formal dinner; or serve with a sandwich for an easygoing lunch.

- 1 **package (about 10 oz.) frozen chopped spinach**
- 4 **cups low-sodium chicken broth**
- 2 **tablespoons grated lemon peel**
- 2 **tablespoons cornstarch**
- 2 **cups buttermilk**
  Salt and pepper

Combine spinach and 2 cups of the broth in a 3- to 4-quart pan. Bring to a boil over high heat, using a spoon to break spinach apart. As soon as you have broken spinach into chunks, pour broth-spinach mixture into a blender; add 1 tablespoon of the lemon peel and whirl until smoothly puréed.

In pan, mix remaining 2 cups broth with corn-starch until smooth; add spinach mixture. Bring to a boil over high heat, stirring often. Mix in butter-milk, then pour into 4 bowls or mugs. Sprinkle with remaining 1 tablespoon lemon peel; season to taste with salt and pepper. Makes 4 servings.

*Light as a breeze, Chicken Salad with Kumquats (recipe on page 28)
features fresh mint as a cooling complement to the nippy ginger in the
dressing. Bubbly spritzers are delicious for sipping alongside; just
mix a fruity white wine, carbonated water, and orange slices.*

Salads

Long a favorite for lowfat menus, salads offer a dazzling spectrum of dining pleasures. Our recipes make the most of wholesome fresh fruits and vegetables, enhancing their fine flavors with herbs, spices, and citrus juices—but little if any fat. Some of the choices in this chapter easily qualify as complete meals, since they're fortified with helpings of lean meat, chicken, or seafood. You'll find our dressings delectable not only with the salads for which they're intended, but also with your own combinations of greens, grains, legumes, fruits, and raw or cooked vegetables.

Pictured on page 7

Spiced Pork & Orange Salad

Preparation time: About 45 minutes

Cooking time: About 5 minutes

Bright green spinach leaves frame a warm main-dish salad sparked with garlic and chili. Thinly sliced pork is cooked quickly, then tossed in a cilantro-lime dressing and served on fresh orange slices.

> Cilantro Dressing (recipe follows)
> 5 large oranges (about 3 lbs. *total*)
> About 30 large spinach leaves (about 3 oz. *total*), rinsed and crisped
> 1 teaspoon salad oil
> 1 pound pork tenderloin or boned pork loin, trimmed of fat and cut into ½-inch-wide strips
> 1 tablespoon minced garlic
> 1 teaspoon *each* chili powder and dry oregano
> 1 teaspoon reduced-sodium soy sauce
> Cilantro sprigs

Per serving:
307 **calories** *(14% fat, 51% carbohydrates, 35% protein), 5 g* **total fat** *(1 g saturated), 41 g* **carbohydrates**, *28 g* **protein**, *74 mg* **cholesterol**, *174 mg* **sodium**

Prepare Cilantro Dressing; set aside. Cut peel and white membrane from oranges, then cut fruit crosswise into thin slices. Arrange a fourth each of the orange slices and spinach leaves on each of 4 salad or dinner plates.

Heat oil in a wide frying pan over high heat. Add pork, garlic, chili powder, and oregano. Cook, stirring, until pork is no longer pink in center; cut to test (about 5 minutes). Add Cilantro Dressing and soy sauce; stir to loosen browned bits. Spoon hot pork mixture equally over oranges. Garnish with cilantro sprigs. Makes 4 servings.

Cilantro Dressing. In a small bowl, mix ½ cup **lime juice**, 2 tablespoons **sugar,** and ¼ cup chopped **cilantro.**

Pictured on page 26

Chicken Salad with Kumquats

Preparation time: About 30 minutes

Cooking time: About 25 minutes

Inspired by the cuisine of Vietnam, this light entrée is a refreshingly different version of the popular chicken-and-fruit salad. Bright orange kumquats—sweet on the outside, tart within—accent chicken breast and cucumber in a gingery mint dressing.

> 8 cups water
> 1½ pounds chicken breast halves
> Ginger-Mint Dressing (recipe follows)
> ¾ cup kumquats (about 5 oz.), thinly sliced, seeds and ends discarded
> 1 medium-size cucumber (about 8 oz.), cut in half lengthwise, then thinly sliced crosswise
> 16 Belgian endive spears or 8 large radicchio leaves (about 6 oz. *total*), rinsed and crisped
> Mint sprigs (optional)

Per serving:
218 **calories** *(12% fat, 38% carbohydrates, 50% protein), 3 g* **total fat** *(1 g saturated), 21 g* **carbohydrates**, *28 g* **protein**, *69 mg* **cholesterol**, *225 mg* **sodium**

In a 5- to 6-quart pan, bring water to a boil over high heat. Rinse chicken; add to pan and return to a boil. Cover pan tightly and remove from heat. Let stand until meat in thickest part is no longer pink; cut to test (about 20 minutes).

Lift chicken from pan and let cool. Remove and discard skin and bones from chicken; tear meat into bite-size shreds.

Prepare Ginger-Mint Dressing. Add kumquats to bowl with dressing; mix gently. Mix in cucumber and chicken. Arrange endive spears or radicchio leaves around edge of a platter; spoon chicken mixture in center. Garnish with mint sprigs, if desired. Makes 4 servings.

Ginger-Mint Dressing. In a large bowl, mix ½ cup **lemon juice**, ¼ cup finely shredded **fresh mint** or 2 tablespoons dry mint, 2 tablespoons *each* **water** and finely chopped **crystallized ginger**, 2½ teaspoons **sugar,** and 1 tablespoon **fish sauce** (*nuoc mam* or *nam pla*) or reduced-sodium soy sauce.

Smoked Trout & Onion Salad

Per serving:
192 calories (24% fat, 22% carbohydrates, 54% protein), 5 g total fat (2 g saturated), 10 g carbohydrates, 26 g protein, 75 mg cholesterol, 665 mg sodium

Preparation time: About 30 minutes

Cool greens, crisp red onion, and smoked seafood combine in an appetizing no-cook entrée for a warm day. A smooth dill-horseradish dressing tops each serving.

- 1 **medium-size red onion, thinly sliced**
- ¼ **cup distilled white vinegar**
- 2 **cups** *each* **water and ice cubes**
   Dill Dressing (recipe follows)
- 1 **large head romaine lettuce (about 1¼ lbs.), separated into leaves, rinsed, and crisped**
- 12 **ounces boneless, skinless smoked trout fillets, torn into ½-inch pieces**
   Dill sprigs (optional)

Place onion slices in a deep bowl and cover with water. With your hands, squeeze slices until they are almost limp. Drain, rinse, and drain again.

In same bowl, combine onion slices, vinegar, and the 2 cups *each* water and ice cubes; let stand until onion is crisp (about 15 minutes). Drain onion well, then lift to a large bowl.

Prepare Dill Dressing; set aside.

Line each of 4 salad or dinner plates with 2 or 3 large lettuce leaves. Cut remaining lettuce crosswise into ¼-inch-wide strips. Add lettuce and trout to bowl with onion; mix gently.

Mound equal portions of salad on each plate; spoon Dill Dressing evenly over salads. Garnish with dill sprigs, if desired. Makes 4 servings.

Dill Dressing. In a small bowl, mix ½ cup **reduced-fat sour cream,** 1 tablespoon **lemon juice,** 2 teaspoons **prepared horseradish,** and 1 teaspoon chopped **fresh dill** or 1 teaspoon dry dill weed.

Mizuna, Fennel & Crab Salad

Per serving:
173 calories (20% fat, 17% carbohydrates, 63% protein), 4 g total fat (1 g saturated), 7 g carbohydrates, 27 g protein, 117 mg cholesterol, 469 mg sodium

Preparation time: About 15 minutes

Pleasantly pungent mizuna, one of the milder members of the mustard family, stars in this hearty main-course salad. You combine the cut-up leaves with fennel and sweet crabmeat, then top the mixture with a tart dressing featuring the puréed greens. Look for mizuna in Asian and specialty produce stores; some supermarkets also carry it.

- 12 **ounces fennel**
- ⅔ **pound mizuna, bare stems trimmed, leaves rinsed and crisped**
   Mizuna Dressing (recipe follows)
- 1½ **pounds cooked crabmeat**

Cut feathery tops from fennel; set aside for dressing. Cut root ends and any bruised spots from fennel head; then thinly slice fennel (you should have 2 cups) and place in a large bowl.

Reserve ¾ cup of the mizuna for dressing. Cut remaining mizuna into 2- to 3-inch-long pieces; place in bowl with sliced fennel.

Prepare Mizuna Dressing; set aside.

Mound crab on mizuna mixture in bowl, placing the most attractive crab pieces on top. At the table, add Mizuna Dressing to salad; mix gently. Makes 6 servings.

Mizuna Dressing. In a blender or food processor, combine the ¾ cup **reserved mizuna,** ⅔ cup **plain nonfat yogurt,** ¼ cup **reduced-fat sour cream,** 2 tablespoons **lemon juice,** 1 tablespoon *each* **Dijon mustard** and chopped **reserved fennel leaves,** 1 teaspoon **dry tarragon,** and ½ teaspoon **sugar.** Whirl until puréed.

Shrimp & Spinach Slaw

Per serving:
103 *calories* (20% fat, 30% carbohydrates, 50% protein), 2 g *total fat* (1 g saturated), 8 g *carbohydrates*, 13 g *protein*, 100 mg *cholesterol*, 192 mg *sodium*

Preparation time: About 25 minutes

For your next barbecue, forget the familiar and prepare a new version of coleslaw: fresh spinach, tiny shrimp, and shredded cabbage tossed in a tart lemon dressing.

   4 **cups finely shredded green cabbage (about 1 lb.)**
   3 **cups thinly sliced spinach leaves (about 4 oz.)**
   1 **medium-size cucumber (8 to 10 oz.), peeled and thinly sliced**
   2 **medium-size celery stalks, thinly sliced**
     Yogurt-Lemon Dressing (recipe follows)
     About 12 large spinach leaves, rinsed and crisped (optional)
   ¾ **to 1 pound small cooked shrimp**
     Lemon wedges (optional)
     Salt and pepper

In a large bowl, combine cabbage, sliced spinach leaves, cucumber, and celery. (At this point, you may cover and refrigerate until next day.)

Prepare Yogurt-Lemon Dressing; add to salad and mix well. If using large spinach leaves, use them to garnish salad in bowl; or arrange them around rim of a large platter and mound salad in center. Sprinkle shrimp over salad. If desired, offer lemon wedges to squeeze over salad; season to taste with salt and pepper. Makes 8 servings.

Yogurt-Lemon Dressing. In a small bowl, mix ⅔ cup **plain nonfat yogurt**, 3 tablespoons **reduced-calorie mayonnaise**, ½ cup thinly sliced **green onions**, 1 teaspoon **grated lemon peel**, 2 tablespoons **lemon juice**, and 1 tablespoon **sugar**. If made ahead, cover and refrigerate until next day.

Pictured on facing page

Bulgur & Hominy Salad

Per serving:
197 *calories* (11% fat, 78% carbohydrates, 11% protein), 2 g *total fat* (0.4 g saturated), 40 g *carbohydrates*, 6 g *protein*, 0 mg *cholesterol*, 270 mg *sodium*

Preparation time: About 15 minutes

Standing time: About 30 minutes

Chilling time: At least 2 hours

Next time you're asked to bring a salad to a summer party, try this filling combination of golden hominy and cracked wheat, seasoned with mustard and fennel seeds and topped with juicy grapes.

   2 **cups low-sodium chicken broth**
   1 **tablespoon mustard seeds**
   1 **teaspoon dry thyme**
   ½ **teaspoon fennel seeds**
   1 **cup bulgur (cracked wheat)**
   ¼ **cup sherry vinegar or red wine vinegar**
   1 **tablespoon rinsed, drained green peppercorns**
   2 **cans (about 14½ oz. *each*) golden hominy, drained**
   ¼ **cup minced parsley**
     Salt
     Napa cabbage leaves, rinsed and crisped (optional)
   ½ **to 1 cup thinly sliced red radishes**
   1 **to 1½ cups seedless green grapes**

In a 1- to 1½-quart pan, combine broth, mustard seeds, thyme, and fennel seeds. Bring to a boil over high heat; stir in bulgur, vinegar, and green peppercorns. Cover, remove from heat, and let stand until bulgur is tender to bite (about 30 minutes). Pour mixture into a bowl; stir in hominy, cover, and refrigerate for at least 2 hours or up to 2 days.

Mix parsley into salad; season to taste with salt. Mound salad onto a platter; or, if desired, line a bowl with cabbage leaves and spoon in salad. Top with radishes and grapes. Makes 6 to 8 servings.

Wreathed with green grapes and crisp radishes, Bulgur & Hominy Salad
(recipe on facing page) is a refreshing contribution to a picnic or potluck. Try
it with barbecued chicken, turkey, or lean beef top round.

Indonesian Rice Salad

Per serving:
212 calories (8% fat, 83% carbohydrates, 9% protein), 2 g total fat (0.3 g saturated), 44 g carbohydrates, 5 g protein, 0 mg cholesterol, 159 mg sodium

Preparation time: About 20 minutes

Cooking time: About 45 minutes

Red bell pepper, snow peas, and water chestnuts add color and crunch to this brown rice salad. Dressed with a light sesame-oil vinaigrette, it's a super accompaniment for meat, fish, or poultry.

   2 **cups long-grain brown rice**
 4½ **cups water**
      Lime Dressing (recipe follows)
  ⅓ **pound Chinese pea pods (also called snow peas), ends and strings removed**
   1 **medium-size red or green bell pepper (about 6 oz.), seeded and chopped**
   5 **green onions, thinly sliced**
   1 **can (about 8 oz.) water chestnuts, drained and chopped**
  ¼ **cup chopped cilantro**
  ¼ **cup raisins (optional)**

In a 2½- to 3-quart pan, combine rice and water. Bring to a boil over high heat; then reduce heat, cover, and simmer until rice is tender to bite (about 45 minutes). Let cool, uncovered, in pan. Meanwhile, prepare Lime Dressing.

Thinly slice pea pods. Place in a large bowl; add bell pepper, onions, water chestnuts, cilantro, raisins (if desired), rice, and Lime Dressing. Mix to blend. Spoon salad into a shallow serving bowl. Makes 8 servings.

Lime Dressing. In a small bowl, mix ⅔ cup **rice or cider vinegar,** 2 tablespoons *each* **reduced-sodium soy sauce** and **lime juice,** 1 tablespoon minced **fresh ginger,** 2 teaspoons minced **garlic,** and 1 teaspoon **Oriental sesame oil** or salad oil.

Fruited Quinoa Salad

Per serving:
359 calories (14% fat, 76% carbohydrates, 10% protein), 6 g total fat (1 g saturated), 72 g carbohydrates, 10 g protein, 0 mg cholesterol, 60 mg sodium

Preparation time: About 15 minutes

Cooking time: About 25 minutes

Wholesome, high-protein quinoa is a great addition to your diet. Rinse the grain carefully to remove its slightly bitter coating; then cook it in a lemon-scented broth and mix it with dried apricots and currants.

  ¼ **cup pine nuts or slivered almonds**
 2½ **cups dried apricots (about 1 lb.)**
   3 **cups quinoa**
   1 **tablespoon salad oil**
   6 **cups low-sodium chicken broth**
   4 **teaspoons grated lemon peel**
  ¼ **cup lemon juice**
   2 **cups dried currants**
      Salt

Toast pine nuts in a small frying pan over medium heat until golden brown (about 3 minutes), shaking pan often. Remove from pan and set aside. Coarsely chop 1 cup of the apricots; set aside.

Place quinoa in a fine strainer and rinse well with cool water. Heat oil in a wide frying pan or 4- to 5-quart pan over medium heat. Add quinoa and cook, stirring often, until grain turns a slightly darker brown (about 8 minutes).

To pan, add broth, lemon peel, and lemon juice. Bring to a boil over high heat; reduce heat, cover, and simmer until quinoa is just tender to bite (about 10 minutes). Drain quinoa; then stir in chopped apricots and 1 cup of the currants. Let stand until warm or cool. If made ahead, cover and refrigerate until next day; before serving, let stand at room temperature until no longer cold.

To serve, mound salad in center of a large rimmed platter. Garnish with pine nuts, remaining 1½ cups apricots, and remaining 1 cup currants. Season to taste with salt. Makes 12 servings.

Viennese Potato Salad

Per serving:
307 *calories* (29% fat, 65% carbohydrates, 6% protein), 10 g *total fat* (1 g saturated), 51 g *carbohydrates*, 4 g *protein*, 0 mg *cholesterol*, 15 mg *sodium*

Preparation time: About 30 minutes

Cooking time: About 40 minutes

Our poppy seed–speckled potato salad boasts red-skinned apples, toasted pecans, sweet raisins, and a simple dressing of fruity late-harvest wine and tart cider vinegar.

- 2½ **pounds small red thin-skinned potatoes (*each* about 1½ inches in diameter), scrubbed**
- ½ **cup pecan or walnut pieces**
- 3 **large red-skinned apples such as Red Gravenstein or Red Delicious (about 1½ lbs. *total*)**
- ½ **cup sliced green onions**
- ⅓ **cup raisins**
- ⅓ **cup late-harvest Gewürztraminer or Johannisberg Riesling**
- ⅓ **cup cider vinegar**
- 2 **tablespoons salad oil**
- 1 **tablespoon grated lemon peel**
- 2 **teaspoons poppy seeds**

Place potatoes in a 4- to 5-quart pan and add enough water to barely cover. Bring water to just below a boil over medium-high heat; then reduce heat, cover, and simmer until potatoes are tender when pierced (about 30 minutes). Drain and let cool; cut into 1-inch cubes and set aside.

Toast pecans in a wide frying pan over medium-high heat until lightly browned and fragrant (about 3 minutes), shaking pan often. Remove from pan and let cool; chop coarsely and set aside.

Core 2 of the apples and cut fruit into 1-inch chunks. In a large bowl, combine apple chunks, potatoes, pecans, onions, raisins, wine, vinegar, oil, lemon peel, and poppy seeds; mix gently. If made ahead, cover and refrigerate for up to 6 hours.

To serve, mound salad on a large rimmed platter. Core remaining apple and cut into slices; fan slices out next to salad along one side of platter. Makes 6 to 8 servings.

Summer Fruit & Almond Salad

Per serving:
128 *calories* (28% fat, 62% carbohydrates, 10% protein), 4 g *total fat* (0.4 g saturated), 21 g *carbohydrates*, 3 g *protein*, 0 mg *cholesterol*, 12 mg *sodium*

Preparation time: About 45 minutes

Cooking time: About 3 minutes

Celebrate summer's bounty with color, flavor, and style: serve a rainbow of melons, grapes, and berries in a slightly sweet, almond-flavored citrus dressing.

- ½ **cup sliced almonds**
- 8 **ounces jicama, peeled and cut into matchstick pieces**
- ¼ **cup orange juice**
- 2 **tablespoons lemon juice**
- 1 **teaspoon *each* poppy seeds and sugar**
- ¼ **teaspoon almond extract**
- 2 **cups cubed, seeded watermelon**
- 2 **cups cubed cantaloupe**
- 1 **cup seedless grapes, halved**
- 1 **cup strawberries, hulled and sliced**
- 12 **to 16 large lettuce leaves, rinsed and crisped**
- 1 **large kiwi fruit (about 4 oz.)**

Toast almonds in a wide frying pan over medium-high heat until golden brown (about 3 minutes), shaking pan often. Remove from pan and set aside.

In a large bowl, mix jicama, orange juice, lemon juice, poppy seeds, sugar, and almond extract. Add watermelon, cantaloupe, grapes, and strawberries; mix gently.

Arrange lettuce leaves on 6 to 8 salad plates; evenly mound fruit mixture on lettuce. Peel and thinly slice kiwi fruit. Garnish salad with kiwi fruit and almonds. Makes 6 to 8 servings.

Seasoned with a spicy hoisin marinade, tender Roast Beef with Couscous (recipe on page 36) is a superb choice for a company dinner. Serve steamed baby French carrots—or carrots of any size and shape— atop the fluffy and flavorful couscous.

Meats

Lean meats merit a leading role in your meal planning. In this chapter, we focus on cuts of beef, lamb, pork, and veal that bring you the most flavor for the least fat. Shop carefully for the leanest possible steaks, chops, and roasts; trim any surface fat, then use cooking fat sparingly. We often rely on techniques that let you omit fat entirely: oven-browning and braise-deglazing, for example. As a general rule, offer meats in judicious portions (about 3 ounces per serving), then complement them with appetizing fat-free side dishes such as crusty whole-grain breads, fresh fruits and vegetables, and grains like bulgur, couscous, and brown rice.

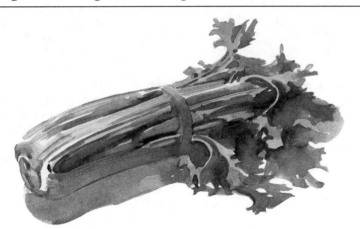

Pictured on page 34

Roast Beef with Couscous

Per serving:
*429 **calories** (15% fat, 44% carbohydrates, 41% protein), 7 g **total fat** (2 g saturated), 46 g **carbohydrates**, 42 g **protein**, 95 mg **cholesterol**, 682 mg **sodium***

Preparation time: About 10 minutes

Cooking time: About 45 minutes

For a company-pleasing main dish, coat a lean beef roast with red wine, hoisin sauce, garlic, and coriander; then use the basting sauce and meat juices to flavor the accompanying couscous.

- 1 **boneless beef triangle tip (tri-tip) or top round roast (about 1¾ lbs.), trimmed of fat**
- ½ **cup dry red wine**
- 2 **tablespoons hoisin sauce**
- 2 **cloves garlic, minced or pressed**
- ½ **teaspoon ground coriander**
  About 2¼ cups beef broth
- 1½ **cups couscous**
- 1 **package (about 10 oz.) frozen tiny peas, thawed**
- ¼ **cup sliced green onions**
  Parsley sprigs

Place beef in an 8- by 12-inch roasting pan. In a small bowl, mix wine, hoisin sauce, garlic, and coriander; brush evenly over beef. Roast in a 425° oven until a meat thermometer inserted in thickest part of roast registers 135°F for rare (about 35 minutes; after 25 minutes, check temperature every 5 minutes). During roasting, brush beef 4 times with wine mixture. If pan drippings begin to burn, add 4 to 6 tablespoons water to pan and stir to loosen browned bits.

Transfer beef to a board and cover loosely. Combine any remaining wine mixture and all the pan juices, then measure; add enough broth to make 2¼ cups total. Pour broth mixture into roasting pan; bring to a boil, stirring to loosen browned bits. Add couscous; return to a boil, stirring. Remove pan from heat, cover tightly with foil, and let stand until liquid is absorbed (about 5 minutes). Stir in peas, onions, and any juices that have accumulated around beef.

Arrange beef and couscous on a warm platter; garnish with parsley sprigs. Makes 4 to 6 servings.

Steak & Spaghetti

Per serving:
*456 **calories** (9% fat, 64% carbohydrates, 27% protein), 4 g **total fat** (1 g saturated), 73 g **carbohydrates**, 30 g **protein**, 43 mg **cholesterol**, 522 mg **sodium***

Preparation time: About 15 minutes

Cooking time: About 2 hours and 50 minutes

Beef chunks, tomatoes, mushrooms, carrots, and onion bake slowly together, demanding next to no attention from the cook. To serve the hearty casserole, just spoon it over hot pasta.

- 1 **pound boneless beef top round, trimmed of fat and cut into 1-inch cubes**
- 3 **tablespoons all-purpose flour**
- 1½ **cups beef broth**
- ½ **cup dry white wine**
- 1 **large onion, chopped**
- 2 **teaspoons minced or pressed garlic**
- 1 **large carrot (about 4 oz.), sliced**
- 8 **ounces mushrooms, sliced**
- ¼ **cup tomato paste**
- 2 **tablespoons chopped parsley**
- 2 **teaspoons dry oregano**
- 1 **can (about 14½ oz.) stewed tomatoes**
- 1 **pound dry spaghetti**

Coat beef cubes with flour; set slightly apart in an ungreased shallow 3- to 3½-quart baking dish. Bake in a 500° oven for 20 minutes; remove from oven and let cool in dish for 5 minutes.

Reduce oven temperature to 350°. Add broth and wine to beef in baking dish; stir to loosen browned bits. Stir in onion, garlic, carrot, mushrooms, tomato paste, parsley, and oregano. Cut up tomatoes; add tomatoes and their liquid to dish. Cover tightly and bake until beef is very tender when pierced (about 2½ hours).

When beef is almost done, in a 6- to 8-quart pan, cook spaghetti in about 4 quarts boiling water until tender to bite (about 10 minutes); or cook according to package directions. Drain well. Serve meat sauce over hot pasta. Makes 6 servings.

Grilled Beef Pocket Sandwiches

Per serving:
427 **calories** *(24% fat, 45% carbohydrates, 31% protein),*
11 g **total fat** *(3 g saturated), 47 g* **carbohydrates**, *33 g*
protein, *76 mg* **cholesterol**, *952 mg* **sodium**

Preparation time: About 15 minutes

Marinating time: At least 30 minutes

Grilling time: About 4 minutes

Easy to assemble and easy to eat, these sandwiches
will be walk-away winners at your next barbecue.
Guests fill pita bread halves with fresh cilantro,
grilled bell peppers, and tender beef strips basted
with a lively soy marinade.

- 1½ **pounds tender beef steak such as top
  sirloin, cut about 1 inch thick**
- 1 **large clove garlic**
- ½ **small onion, cut into chunks**
- 2 **tablespoons** *each* **sugar, water, salad oil,
  and lemon juice**
- ⅓ **cup reduced-sodium soy sauce**
- 2 **large red bell peppers (about 1 lb.** *total*),
  seeded and cut into 1½-inch squares
- 6 **pita breads (***each* **about 6 inches in
  diameter), halved**
- 2 **cups lightly packed cilantro sprigs,
  rinsed and crisped**

Trim fat from beef; then cut meat into long, ¼-inch-
thick slices. In a blender or food processor, combine garlic, onion, sugar, water, oil, lemon juice,
and soy sauce; whirl until puréed. Pour into a
bowl; mix in beef and bell peppers. Cover and refrigerate for at least 30 minutes or until next day.

Drain marinade from beef and peppers; reserve. Thread beef strips alternately with pepper
squares on thin metal skewers. (To thread each beef
strip, pierce one end of strip with skewer; then fold
strip back and forth several times, piercing each time.
Threaded meat will have a "rippled" look.) Place
skewers on a grill 4 to 6 inches above a solid bed of
medium-hot coals. Cook, turning often and basting
with marinade, until beef is done medium-rare; cut
to test (about 4 minutes).

To eat, fill pita bread halves with beef, bell peppers, and cilantro sprigs. Makes 6 servings.

Veal Chops & Sage Dressing

Per serving:
349 **calories** *(13% fat, 59% carbohydrates, 28% protein), 5 g*
total fat *(1 g saturated), 53 g* **carbohydrates**, *25 g* **protein**,
80 mg **cholesterol**, *299 mg* **sodium**

Preparation time: About 15 minutes

Cooking time: About 45 minutes

Treat family and friends to a tempting meal: juicy
veal chops topped with a sage-seasoned apple
dressing, then simmered to tenderness in white
wine and chicken broth.

- 1 **large onion, chopped**
- 1½ **cups low-sodium chicken broth**
- 4 **cups cubed whole wheat bread (½-inch
  cubes; you need 4 or 5 slices)**
- 2 **stalks celery, thinly sliced**
- 1 **large tart green-skinned apple such as
  Granny Smith or Newtown Pippin (about
  8 oz.), cored and chopped**
- 1 **cup raisins**
- 1 **teaspoon dry sage**
- 4 **veal loin chops (about 1½ lbs.** *total*),
  trimmed of fat
- ½ **cup dry white wine**

Place onion and ½ cup of the broth in a wide nonstick frying pan. Cook over high heat, stirring
often, until onion is soft and liquid has evaporated
(about 5 minutes). Scrape onion into a large bowl;
add ½ cup more broth, bread, celery, apple, raisins,
and sage. Mix until well blended.

Add veal chops to pan and cook over medium-
high heat, turning once, until well browned on
both sides (about 5 minutes). Pile dressing evenly
over chops. Pour wine and remaining ½ cup broth
around chops; bring to a boil. Reduce heat to low,
cover, and simmer until veal is very tender when
pierced (about 35 minutes). Makes 4 servings.

Braised Veal Shanks

Per serving:
268 calories (16% fat, 7% carbohydrates, 77% protein), 5 g total fat (1 g saturated), 4 g carbohydrates, 50 g protein, 177 mg cholesterol, 696 mg sodium

Preparation time: About 10 minutes

Cooking time: About 2¼ hours

Oven-browning and long baking ensure meat that's both tender and richly flavored. Gravy made from the seasoned pan juices is a delicious extra.

> 6 **veal shanks,** *each* **about 6 inches long (about 6 lbs.** *total***); have your butcher split each shank in half crosswise**
>
> 1 **lemon (unpeeled), chopped**
>
> 4 **cups beef broth**
>
> 1 **teaspoon dry marjoram**
>
> 1 **dry bay leaf**
>
> ½ **teaspoon whole black peppercorns**
>
> ¼ **teaspoon coriander seeds**
>
> 2 **tablespoons balsamic or red wine vinegar**
>
> 1 **tablespoon cornstarch mixed with 2 tablespoons cold water**

Lay veal in a single layer in a 9- by 13-inch baking pan. Bake in a 400° oven until browned (about 35 minutes). Remove pan from oven; turn veal over. Then add lemon, broth, marjoram, bay leaf, peppercorns, and coriander seeds to pan. Cover tightly with foil, return to oven, and bake until meat is so tender it pulls apart easily (about 1½ hours).

With a slotted spoon, lift veal shanks gently to a warm platter; keep warm.

Pour pan juices through a fine strainer into a 1-quart measure; press residue in strainer to extract any liquid. Discard residue. (At this point, you may cover and refrigerate veal and pan juices separately until next day. Before continuing, reheat veal, covered, in a 400° oven until warm—15 to 20 minutes. Place on a warm platter; keep warm.)

Skim and discard fat from pan juices (or lift off and discard solidified fat from chilled juices). Pour pan juices into a wide frying pan; add vinegar and bring to a boil over high heat. Boil, uncovered, until reduced to 1½ to 2 cups (8 to 12 minutes). Stir in cornstarch mixture and return to a boil, stirring.

Pour gravy into a small pitcher; offer at the table to pour over meat to taste. Makes 6 servings.

Pictured on facing page

Roast Pork with Date & Fig Sauce

Per serving:
342 calories (25% fat, 44% carbohydrates, 31% protein), 10 g total fat (3 g saturated), 37 g carbohydrates, 26 g protein, 74 mg cholesterol, 86 mg sodium

Preparation time: About 15 minutes

Cooking time: About 1 hour and 35 minutes

Turn Sunday supper into something special with this creative meat-and-fruit combination. Pork roast is seasoned with garlic, pepper, and savory, then served with a sweet sauce of figs, dates, and fresh apple.

> 1 **boned pork loin roast (3 to 4 lbs.), trimmed of fat**
>
> 1 **clove garlic, halved**
>
> ½ **teaspoon dry summer savory**
>
> 1 **teaspoon pepper**
>
> 1 **cup finely chopped unpeeled tart apple**
>
> ¼ **cup water**
>
> ½ **cup dry white wine**
>
> ½ **cup firmly packed brown sugar**
>
> 1 **cup pitted dates, cut into pieces**
>
> 6 **dried figs, coarsely chopped**

Rub pork all over with cut garlic; discard garlic. Place pork in a 9- by 13-inch baking pan and sprinkle evenly with savory and pepper. Roast in a 375° oven until a meat thermometer inserted in thickest part registers 155°F (about 1½ hours). Transfer pork to a warm platter; keep warm.

While pork is roasting, combine apple and water in a 2- to 3-quart pan. Cover and cook over medium heat until apple is tender to bite (about 5 minutes). Remove from heat; set aside.

Skim and discard fat from juices in roasting pan; add wine to pan and place over medium heat, stirring to loosen browned bits. Add apple mixture, sugar, dates, and figs; cook, stirring, until sauce is hot (about 3 minutes). Pour into a small bowl; serve with pork. Makes 8 to 10 servings.

*Dried fruits and a chopped fresh apple bring rich autumn flavors to
Roast Pork with Date & Fig Sauce (recipe on facing page). Complement the
lean meat and its wine-accented sauce with fluffy mashed sweet potatoes,
steamed broccoli, and a blush wine such as white zinfandel.*

Pork Tenderloin with Bulgur

Per serving:
350 calories (24% fat, 34% carbohydrates, 42% protein), 9 g total fat (2 g saturated), 29 g carbohydrates, 36 g protein, 89 mg cholesterol, 504 mg sodium

Preparation time: About 10 minutes

Cooking time: About 30 minutes

By taking advantage of quick-cooking pork tenderloin, you can have a complete meal on the table in little more than half an hour. The pan-browned meat is served with bulgur, asparagus, and a red wine sauce that's flavored with balsamic vinegar.

- 3 cups beef broth
- 1 cup bulgur (cracked wheat)
- ½ cup sliced green onions
- 1½ pounds pork tenderloin (about 2 tenderloins), trimmed of fat
- 2 teaspoons sugar
- 1 tablespoon salad oil
- 1 tablespoon *each* mustard seeds and balsamic vinegar
- 2 teaspoons minced fresh oregano or 1 teaspoon dry oregano
- ½ cup dry red wine
- 2 teaspoons cornstarch mixed with 2 teaspoons cold water
- 1 pound asparagus, tough ends broken off
  Salt and pepper

In a 2- to 3-quart pan, bring 2 cups of the broth to a boil; stir in bulgur. Cover, remove from heat, and let stand until bulgur is tender to bite (about 30 minutes). Stir in onions.

While bulgur is standing, sprinkle pork with sugar. Heat oil in a wide frying pan over medium-high heat; add pork and cook, turning as needed, until browned on all sides (about 4 minutes). Add ⅔ cup of the broth, mustard seeds, vinegar, and oregano. Cover, reduce heat to medium-low, and simmer just until meat is no longer pink in center; cut to test (about 12 minutes).

Lift pork to a warm platter and keep warm. To pan, add wine and remaining ⅓ cup broth. Bring to a boil over high heat; then boil until reduced to ¾ cup (about 2 minutes). Stir in cornstarch mixture; return to a boil, stirring.

While sauce is boiling, bring ½ inch of water to a boil in another wide frying pan over high heat. Add asparagus and cook, uncovered, just until barely tender when pierced (about 4 minutes). Drain.

Slice pork; mound bulgur mixture alongside, then top with asparagus. Spoon sauce over meat. Season to taste with salt and pepper. Makes 4 to 6 servings.

Pork Stir-fry with Apple

Per serving:
505 calories (23% fat, 54% carbohydrates, 23% protein), 13 g total fat (4 g saturated), 67 g carbohydrates, 29 g protein, 68 mg cholesterol, 378 mg sodium

Preparation time: About 20 minutes

Marinating time: At least 15 minutes

Cooking time: About 6 minutes

Have the rice ready—this meal cooks in minutes! Make your own tangy teriyaki sauce with fresh ginger, mint, and orange juice; you can marinate the pork while the rice simmers.

- Teriyaki Sauce (recipe on facing page)
- 1 pound boned pork loin or shoulder (butt), trimmed of fat
- 2 medium-size red-skinned apples such as Red Gravenstein or Red Delicious (about 12 oz. *total*), cored and chopped
- 2 tablespoons lemon juice
- 1 tablespoon salad oil
- 1 small onion, cut into thin wedges
- 3 cups hot cooked rice
- 1 or 2 medium-size oranges (peeled, if desired), sliced crosswise
  Mint sprigs (optional)

Prepare Teriyaki Sauce; set aside.

Slice pork across the grain into ¹⁄₁₆- to ⅛-inch-thick strips about 2 inches long. Add pork to Teriyaki Sauce in bowl; cover and refrigerate for at least 15 minutes or until next day. Mix apples with lemon juice; set aside.

Heat oil in a wok or wide frying pan over high heat. Add onion; cook, stirring, until soft (about 2 minutes). Add apples; cook, stirring, until hot (about 1 minute). Spoon mixture into a bowl and set aside.

With a slotted spoon, transfer pork to pan; reserve Teriyaki Sauce in bowl. Cook, stirring, until meat is lightly browned (about 2 minutes). Return apple mixture to pan, then add any remaining Teriyaki Sauce and bring to a boil, stirring.

Mound rice on a warm platter. Pour pork mixture over rice; garnish with orange slices and, if desired, mint sprigs. Makes 4 servings.

Teriyaki Sauce. In a medium-size bowl, mix ½ cup **orange juice**, ¼ cup minced **fresh mint**, 2 tablespoons **reduced-sodium soy sauce**, 1 tablespoon minced **fresh ginger**, and 1 clove **garlic**, minced or pressed.

Per serving:
272 calories (19% fat, 44% carbohydrates, 37% protein), 6 g total fat (2 g saturated), 30 g carbohydrates, 26 g protein, 76 mg cholesterol, 157 mg sodium

Grilled Leg of Lamb & Pears

Preparation time: About 30 minutes

Marinating time: At least 2 hours

Cooking time: About 1 hour and 5 minutes

This combination of butterflied leg of lamb and pears is certain to make any barbecue memorable. Before grilling, both meat and fruit are soaked in a piquant orange-onion marinade that doubles as a tart relish.

Onion Relish Marinade (recipe follows)

5 or 6 large firm-ripe **pears** (about 8 oz. *each*), peeled, halved, and cored

1 **leg of lamb** (about 6 lbs.), boned and trimmed of fat

Salt and pepper

Prepare Onion Relish Marinade and bring to a boil over high heat. Add pears; reduce heat, cover, and simmer, turning fruit over occasionally, until tender when pierced (about 10 minutes).

With a slotted spoon, gently transfer pears to a bowl. Pour about a fourth of the pan liquid through a strainer over pears; return solids in strainer to pan. Cover pears and refrigerate for at least 2 hours or until next day, turning fruit over occasionally.

Meanwhile, place lamb, boned side up, on a board; cut long, deep slashes through thickest sections and press apart to give meat an even thickness. Place lamb in a large bowl; add remaining Onion Relish Marinade from pear cooking pan. Cover and refrigerate for at least 2 hours or until next day, turning lamb over several times.

Lift lamb from marinade; shake off seasonings. Set lamb aside. Transfer marinade left in bowl to a 4- to 5-quart pan; then drain liquid from pears into pan. Bring to a boil over high heat; boil, uncovered, stirring often, until mixture is reduced to about 2½ cups and almost all liquid has evaporated (about 10 minutes). Pour this onion relish into a small bowl.

Lay lamb out flat, boned side up, on a grill over a solid bed of hot coals. Scatter 10 charcoal briquets onto coals. Cook, turning as needed, until lamb is evenly browned and done to your liking; cut in thickest part to test (about 45 minutes for medium-rare).

About 15 minutes before lamb is done, thread pear halves, cut sides up, onto parallel thin metal skewers (this keeps fruit from spinning). Lay pears on grill and cook, turning several times, until warm (about 15 minutes).

Transfer lamb and pears to a large warm platter. Slice lamb; serve with pears and onion relish. Season to taste with salt and pepper. Makes 10 to 12 servings.

Onion Relish Marinade. With a vegetable peeler or sharp knife, remove peel (colored part only) from 1 medium-size **orange**. Finely chop peel and place in a 4- to 5-quart pan. Cut off and discard remaining peel and white membrane. Holding orange over pan, cut between membranes to free segments; drop segments into pan. Squeeze juice from membranes into pan; discard membranes.

To pan, add 1 large **red onion**, minced; 2 cups **dry red wine**; ½ cup **beef broth**; ½ cup **golden or dark raisins**; ¼ cup *each* **raspberry vinegar** and **balsamic vinegar** (or all raspberry vinegar); 2 tablespoons minced **fresh ginger**; ¼ cup **sugar**; and 1 tablespoon **Dijon mustard**.

This robust casserole draws its inspiration from Mexico's southeastern coast. Yucatán Tamale Pie (recipe on page 44) features a spicy filling that's thick with chicken and tomatoes; on top goes a ring of golden biscuits, made with masa harina for tempting tortilla flavor.

Poultry

When you're on the lookout for lowfat main dishes, put
poultry entrées at the top of your list. There's not much fat
in either chicken or turkey—just plenty of great taste. You'll
find appealing diversity in the recipes we present here, from
comforting family fare such as Yucatán Tamale Pie and
Creamy Baked Turkey & Rotelle to elegant Chicken Breasts
Calvados and exotic Saffron & Honey Chicken. When you
prepare chicken and turkey, remove and discard the skin
before cooking. This simple procedure not only banishes fat,
but also allows the meat to better absorb the flavors of
herbs, spices, and savory cooking liquids.

Pictured on page 42

Yucatán Tamale Pie

Per serving:
316 **calories** (29% fat, 38% carbohydrates, 33% protein), 10 g **total fat** (2 g saturated), 30 g **carbohydrates**, 26 g **protein**, 63 mg **cholesterol**, 215 mg **sodium**

Preparation time: About 35 minutes

Cooking time: About 50 minutes

This deep-dish version of tamale pie boasts masa biscuits baked atop a richly flavored chicken filling. Achiote condiment is sold in Hispanic markets and some well-stocked supermarkets; if you can't find it, use our easy-to-make substitute.

- 3 **ounces achiote condiment or substitute (recipe follows)**
- 2 **cups low-sodium chicken broth**
- 2 **tablespoons minced fresh mint or 1 teaspoon dry mint**
- ⅛ **teaspoon anise seeds**
- 3 **cups bite-size pieces of cooked chicken**
- 2 **large onions, chopped**
- 2 **large tomatoes (about 1 lb. *total*), cored and cut into wedges**
- 2 **tablespoons cornstarch mixed with ¼ cup cold water**
  Masa Topping (recipe follows)
  Cilantro sprigs

Place achiote condiment (or substitute) in a 2-quart pan; stir in ½ cup of the broth. With a heavy spoon, work mixture into a smooth paste. Stir in remaining 1½ cups broth, mint, and anise seeds. Bring to a boil over high heat. Then reduce heat and simmer, uncovered, for 5 minutes, stirring often to prevent sticking. (At this point, you may let cool, then cover and refrigerate until next day.)

Stir chicken, onions, tomatoes, and cornstarch mixture into achiote mixture; pour into a deep 2- to 3-quart casserole and spread evenly. Prepare Masa Topping; drop in spoonfuls over chicken mixture.

Bake on bottom rack of a 400° oven until filling is bubbly in center and topping is well browned (about 45 minutes). Remove from oven and let stand for 5 minutes before serving. Garnish with cilantro sprigs. Makes 6 servings.

Achiote Substitute. In a small bowl, mix 3 tablespoons **paprika**, 2 tablespoons **distilled white vinegar**, 1½ teaspoons **dry oregano**, 3 cloves **garlic** (minced), and ½ teaspoon **ground cumin.**

Masa Topping. In a small bowl, combine ½ cup *each* **masa harina** (dehydrated masa flour) and **all-purpose flour**. Stir in 1½ teaspoons **baking powder**. Add 1 large **egg white**, 1½ tablespoons **salad oil**, and ½ cup **nonfat milk;** stir just until blended.

Chicken Breasts Calvados

Per serving:
376 **calories** (27% fat, 18% carbohydrates, 55% protein), 10 g **total fat** (5 g saturated), 15 g **carbohydrates**, 46 g **protein**, 128 mg **cholesterol**, 324 mg **sodium**

Preparation time: About 10 minutes

Baking & broiling time: About 34 minutes

Topped with a golden cheese crust and served on applesauce spiked with apple brandy, these tender chicken breasts make a memorable meal for two.

- 1 **large Golden Delicious apple (about 8 oz.), peeled, cored, and thinly sliced**
- ¼ **cup apple brandy, brandy, or apple juice**
- ¼ **teaspoon ground nutmeg**
- 2 **skinned, boned chicken breast halves (about 6 oz. *each*)**
- 2 **slices Havarti cheese (about 1 oz. *each*)**
  Chopped parsley

Divide apple slices between 2 shallow ovenproof 1½- to 2-cup ramekins. Pour 2 tablespoons of the brandy into each ramekin, then sprinkle ⅛ teaspoon of the nutmeg evenly over apples. Cover ramekins tightly with foil and bake in a 400° oven until apples are tender when pierced (about 20 minutes).

Rinse chicken and pat dry. Place one piece in each ramekin; baste with cooking juices, then sprinkle evenly with remaining ⅛ teaspoon nutmeg. Bake, uncovered, until meat in thickest part is no longer pink; cut to test (about 12 minutes).

Top each chicken piece with a cheese slice. Broil 6 inches below heat until cheese is bubbly (about 2 minutes). Sprinkle with parsley. Makes 2 servings.

Mediterranean Baked Chicken & Vegetables

Per serving:
250 calories (21% fat, 19% carbohydrates, 60% protein), 6 g total fat (1 g saturated), 12 g carbohydrates, 38 g protein, 86 mg cholesterol, 270 mg sodium

Preparation time: About 15 minutes

Baking time: About 20 minutes

A fresh-tasting dinner can be on the table quickly when you choose this dish of chicken breasts baked with zucchini, tomatoes, mushrooms, and seasonings of fennel and basil. Serve it over your favorite pasta.

- 4 **chicken breast halves (about 1 lb. *total*), skinned**
- 8 **ounces mushrooms, sliced**
- 1 **pound zucchini, cut into ¼-inch-thick slices**
- 1 **tablespoon olive oil**
- 1 **teaspoon *each* freshly ground pepper and dry oregano**
- 1 **teaspoon fennel seeds, crushed**
- 1 **tablespoon dry basil**
- 1 **can (about 14½ oz.) pear-shaped tomatoes**
  Parsley sprigs
  Grated Parmesan cheese

Rinse chicken, pat dry, and place in a 12- by 15-inch broiler pan. Arrange mushrooms and zucchini around chicken. Drizzle with oil. Sprinkle with pepper, oregano, fennel seeds, and basil; mix to coat chicken and vegetables with seasonings.

Cover pan tightly with foil and bake in a 425° oven for 15 minutes. Cut up tomatoes, then stir tomatoes and their liquid into pan. Cover and continue to bake until meat near bone is no longer pink; cut to test (about 5 more minutes). Garnish with parsley sprigs; offer cheese to sprinkle over individual servings. Makes 4 servings.

Chicken with Onion Marmalade

Per serving:
235 calories (9% fat, 13% carbohydrates, 78% protein), 2 g total fat (1 g saturated), 7 g carbohydrates, 40 g protein, 99 mg cholesterol, 115 mg sodium

Preparation time: About 10 minutes

Marinating time: At least 30 minutes

Cooking time: About 17 minutes

A sweet-tart "marmalade" of red onions, wine, and a little honey covers these sherry-marinated, baked chicken breasts. Serve with brown rice and fresh peas for a fast, flavorful meal.

- 6 **skinned, boned chicken breast halves (about 6 oz. *each*)**
- 3 **tablespoons cream sherry**
- 2 **medium-size red onions**
- ½ **cup dry red wine**
- 1 **tablespoon *each* red wine vinegar and honey**
  Parsley sprigs (optional)
  Salt and pepper

Rinse and drain chicken, then place in a heavy-duty plastic bag and add 2 tablespoons of the sherry. Seal bag; turn to coat chicken with sherry. Refrigerate for at least 30 minutes or up to 6 hours, turning bag over several times.

Meanwhile, thinly slice onions; wrap several slices airtight and refrigerate for up to 6 hours. Combine remaining onion slices, wine, vinegar, and honey in a wide frying pan. Cook over medium-high heat, stirring often, until liquid evaporates. (At this point, you may cover and set aside for up to 6 hours; reheat over medium-high heat, stirring, before proceeding.) Remove from heat and stir in remaining 1 tablespoon sherry.

Remove chicken from bag; arrange in a 9- by 13-inch baking pan. Bake, uncovered, in a 450° oven just until meat in thickest part is no longer pink; cut to test (about 12 minutes). With a slotted spoon, transfer chicken to a warm platter. Spoon onion mixture over chicken. Garnish with reserved onion slices and, if desired, parsley sprigs. Season to taste with salt and pepper. Makes 6 servings.

Pictured on facing page

Chicken Kebabs Shanghai

Per serving:
299 calories (15% fat, 42% carbohydrates, 43% protein), 5 g total fat (1 g saturated), 31 g carbohydrates, 33 g protein, 79 mg cholesterol, 333 mg sodium

Preparation time: About 30 minutes

Marinating time: At least 30 minutes

Broiling time: About 12 minutes

Have a party any time with simple skewers of cubed chicken breast and fresh pineapple chunks; both meat and fruit are flavored with a tangy, ginger-sparked orange marinade. For an attractive presentation, serve asparagus alongside.

- ¾ **teaspoon grated orange peel**
- ⅓ **cup orange juice**
- 3 **tablespoons firmly packed brown sugar**
- 2 **tablespoons reduced-sodium soy sauce**
- 4 **teaspoons** *each* **minced fresh ginger and red wine vinegar**
- 1 **tablespoon Oriental sesame oil or salad oil**
- ½ **teaspoon ground coriander**
- 1½ **pounds skinned, boned chicken breasts, cut into 1½-inch chunks**
- 1 **medium-size pineapple (about 3½ lbs.), peeled, cored, and cut into 1-inch chunks**

In a medium-size bowl, mix orange peel, orange juice, sugar, soy sauce, ginger, vinegar, oil, and coriander. Stir in chicken. Cover and refrigerate for at least 30 minutes or up to 2 hours.

Lift chicken from marinade and drain briefly; reserve marinade. Thread chicken and pineapple chunks on thin metal skewers, alternating 2 chicken chunks and one pineapple chunk. Brush reserved marinade over pineapple. Place skewers on a rack in a 12- by 15-inch broiler pan. Broil about 4 inches below heat, turning once, until chicken is no longer pink in center; cut to test (about 12 minutes). Makes 4 to 6 servings.

Saffron & Honey Chicken

Per serving:
224 calories (25% fat, 18% carbohydrates, 57% protein), 6 g total fat (2 g saturated), 10 g carbohydrates, 31 g protein, 121 mg cholesterol, 212 mg sodium

Preparation time: About 10 minutes

Cooking time: About 55 minutes

Even if no one can figure out all the ingredients in the sauce that tops these richly glazed chicken drumsticks and thighs, everyone's bound to appreciate the flavor!

- ⅔ **cup low-sodium chicken broth**
- 2 **tablespoons** *each* **lime juice and honey**
- ¼ **teaspoon saffron threads**
- 1 **teaspoon white Worcestershire**
- 2 **teaspoons curry powder**
- ½ **teaspoon dry oregano**
- ¼ **teaspoon paprika**
- ⅛ **teaspoon pepper**
- 2 **teaspoons reduced-sodium soy sauce**
- 2 **tablespoons white rice flour mixed with ¼ cup cold water**
- 6 *each* **small chicken drumsticks and thighs (about 2 lbs.** *total***), skinned, fat removed**
  Chopped parsley

In a 1½- to 2-quart pan, mix broth, lime juice, honey, saffron, Worcestershire, curry powder, oregano, paprika, pepper, and soy sauce. Bring to a boil over high heat; then reduce heat and simmer, uncovered, stirring occasionally, until reduced to ½ cup (about 15 minutes). Stir in rice flour mixture; bring to a boil over high heat, stirring. Remove from heat.

Rinse chicken, pat dry, and arrange in a 9- by 13-inch baking pan. Spoon sauce over chicken. Cover pan tightly with foil and bake in a 375° oven until meat near thighbone is no longer pink; cut to test (about 35 minutes). Lift chicken to a warm platter or plates; stir sauce to blend, then spoon evenly over chicken. Sprinkle with parsley. Makes 6 servings.

Juicy with fresh pineapple chunks, orange-accented Chicken
Kebabs Shanghai (recipe on facing page) emerge sizzling hot from the broiler.
Garnish the skewers with shreds of orange peel, if you like; then serve
with steamed asparagus spears and tender brown rice.

Braised Chicken with Green Chile Sauce

Per serving:
269 **calories** *(27% fat, 12% carbohydrates, 61% protein), 8 g* **total fat** *(2 g saturated), 8 g* **carbohydrates**, *40 g* **protein**, *161 mg* **cholesterol**, *351 mg* **sodium**

Preparation time: About 15 minutes

Cooking time: About 40 minutes

Cool weather calls for robust dinner dishes like this one: chicken thighs simmered with bell peppers and mild chiles in an herb-onion base. Serve over rice or in warm flour tortillas, with toppings of yogurt, tomato, and lime.

- 1 **large onion, chopped**
- 2 **cloves garlic, minced or pressed**
- 1 **cup low-sodium chicken broth**
- 1 **teaspoon dry oregano**
- ½ **teaspoon ground cumin**
- 1 **tablespoon red wine vinegar**
- 3 **pounds skinned, boned chicken or turkey thighs, trimmed of fat and cut into 1-inch chunks**
- 2 **large green bell peppers (about 1 lb. *total*), seeded and chopped**
- ½ **cup chopped cilantro**
- 1 **large can (about 7 oz.) diced green chiles**
  Cilantro sprigs
  Hot cooked rice or warm flour tortillas
  Tomato wedges, plain nonfat yogurt or reduced-fat sour cream, and lime wedges
  Salt and pepper

In a 5- to 6-quart pan, combine onion, garlic, broth, oregano, and cumin. Bring to a boil over high heat; boil, stirring occasionally, until liquid evaporates and onion begins to brown (about 10 minutes). To deglaze, add 2 tablespoons water and stir to loosen browned bits. Cook, stirring occasionally, until liquid evaporates and onion begins to brown again. Repeat deglazing step, using 2 tablespoons water each time, until onion is richly browned. Then deglaze one last time with vinegar and 1 tablespoon water.

Stir in chicken, bell peppers, chopped cilantro, chiles, and 1 tablespoon water. Cover and cook over low heat, stirring often, until chicken chunks are no longer pink in center; cut to test (about 15 minutes). Skim and discard fat from sauce.

Spoon chicken mixture into a bowl; garnish with cilantro sprigs. Serve over rice; offer tomato wedges, yogurt, and lime wedges to top each serving. Season to taste with salt and pepper. Makes 6 to 8 servings.

Creamy Baked Turkey & Rotelle

Per serving:
419 **calories** *(23% fat, 50% carbohydrates, 27% protein), 11 g* **total fat** *(4 g saturated), 53 g* **carbohydrates**, *29 g* **protein**, *59 mg* **cholesterol**, *530 mg* **sodium**

Preparation time: About 1½ hours

Baking time: About 20 minutes

You can cater to a crowd and still enjoy the evening if you prepare this pasta dish a day ahead of time. Multicolored rotelle, ground turkey, and zucchini shreds bake in a thyme-accented sauce made with sweet red onions and a little red wine vinegar.

- 3½ **pounds red onions, thinly sliced**
- 3 **ounces Canadian bacon, diced**
- 3 **tablespoons red wine vinegar**
- 1 **pound ground turkey**
- 1 **pound zucchini, shredded**
- 3 **tablespoons minced fresh thyme or 1 tablespoon dry thyme**
- 2 **cups low-sodium chicken broth**
- 1½ **cups nonfat milk**
- 3 **tablespoons cornstarch mixed with ¼ cup cold water**
- 1 **cup (about 4 oz.) shredded Parmesan cheese**
- 10 **ounces dry multicolored rotelle (pasta corkscrews)**

In an 11- by 17-inch roasting pan, combine onions, bacon, and vinegar. Bake, uncovered, in a 400° oven, stirring occasionally, until onions and bacon are well browned (about 55 minutes). Sprinkle turkey, zucchini, and 1 tablespoon of the fresh thyme (or 1 teaspoon of the dry thyme) over onion mixture; continue to bake until turkey just turns white (about 8 more minutes). Transfer turkey mixture to a large bowl.

Add broth, milk, and remaining 2 tablespoons fresh (or 2 teaspoons dry) thyme to roasting pan. Bring to a boil over high heat, stirring to loosen browned bits. Stir in cornstarch mixture; return to a boil, stirring. Remove from heat. Add sauce and ½ cup of the cheese to turkey mixture; mix well.

In a 5- to 6-quart pan, cook rotelle in 3 quarts boiling water until just slightly underdone (about 5 minutes; or cook for two-thirds of the cooking time indicated on package). Drain.

Add pasta to turkey mixture, mix well, and spread in a greased 2- to 2½-quart casserole; sprinkle evenly with remaining ½ cup cheese. (At this point, you may cover and refrigerate until next day.)

Bake, uncovered, in a 400° oven until casserole is browned on top and bubbly in center (about 20 minutes; about 30 minutes if refrigerated). Makes 8 to 10 servings.

Turkey & Lima Stew

Per serving:
*294 calories (23% fat, 27% carbohydrates, 50% protein), 7 g **total fat** (2 g saturated), 20 g **carbohydrates**, 36 g **protein**, 114 mg **cholesterol**, 182 mg **sodium***

Preparation time: About 20 minutes

Cooking time: About 1 hour

Repeated deglazing gives this easy stew its rich color and flavor. Serve over noodles—and don't forget the cranberry sauce!

1 **large onion, chopped**
2 **cups sliced mushrooms**
1 **cup thinly sliced carrots**
1 **teaspoon dry thyme**
   About 3 cups low-sodium chicken broth
2 **tablespoons lemon juice**
2 **pounds skinned, boned turkey or chicken thighs, trimmed of fat and cut into 1-inch chunks**
1 **tablespoon cornstarch**
1 **package (about 10 oz.) frozen baby lima beans, thawed**

In a 5- to 6-quart pan, combine onion, mushrooms, carrots, thyme, and 1 cup of the broth. Bring to a boil over high heat; then boil, uncovered, stirring occasionally, until liquid evaporates and vegetables begin to brown (about 10 minutes). To deglaze, add ¼ cup more broth and stir to loosen browned bits. Cook, stirring occasionally, until liquid evaporates and vegetables begin to brown again. Repeat deglazing step, using ¼ cup more broth each time, about 2 more times or until mixture is richly browned. Then deglaze one last time with lemon juice.

Stir turkey and ½ cup more broth into vegetable mixture. Bring to a boil over high heat. Then reduce heat to low, cover, and simmer until turkey chunks are no longer pink in center; cut to test (about 40 minutes; about 25 minutes for chicken). Skim and discard fat from sauce.

Mix ¾ cup broth and cornstarch. Add cornstarch mixture and beans to pan; bring to a boil over medium-high heat, stirring. Continue to boil, stirring, until beans are tender to bite. Makes 6 servings.

Golden polenta is a staple of Italian country-style cooking—but the corn from which it's made came to Italy from the Americas. As befits its origins, this hearty dish is wonderful with New World seasonings of chile and cumin; in festive Orange Roughy with Polenta (recipe on page 52), it's a flavorful base for mild white fish fillets.

Seafood

As interest in lowfat cooking grows, fish and shellfish

continue to increase in popularity. Naturally low in fat,

seafood is available today in ever wider variety: in addition

to familiar choices like shrimp and salmon, we can savor

such comparatively recent discoveries as orange roughy

from the South Pacific and farm-raised tilapia. Our recipes

reveal resourceful ways with these and other favorites, old

and new. Whether baked, poached, broiled, grilled, or stir-

fried in a nonstick wok or skillet, our seafood selections are

all tempting fare for family or guests.

Pictured on page 50

Orange Roughy with Polenta

Per serving:
328 calories (29% fat, 43% carbohydrates, 28% protein),
10 g total fat (0.7 g saturated), 35 g carbohydrates, 23 g
protein, 23 mg cholesterol, 435 mg sodium

Preparation time: About 10 minutes

Cooking time: About 20 minutes

Brighten up the dinner hour with this quick-to-fix combination. Mild white fish fillets, served on a bed of chile-flecked polenta, are accented with a sprinkling of red bell pepper and green cilantro.

> 1 **cup polenta (Italian-style cornmeal)**
> 4⅓ **cups low-sodium chicken broth**
> ½ **teaspoon cumin seeds**
> 1 **large can (about 7 oz.) diced green chiles**
> 1 **pound boneless, skinless orange roughy fillets, divided into 4 equal-size pieces**
> 1 **medium-size red bell pepper (about 7 oz.), seeded and minced**
> 1 **tablespoon cilantro leaves**
>   **Salt**
>   **Lime wedges**

Pour polenta into a 3- to 4-quart pan; stir in broth and cumin seeds. Bring to a boil over high heat, stirring often with a long-handled wooden spoon (mixture will spatter). Reduce heat and simmer gently, uncovered, stirring often, until polenta tastes creamy (about 20 minutes). Stir in chiles.

When polenta is almost done, rinse and drain fish; then arrange in a 9- by 13-inch baking pan. Bake in a 475° oven until fish is just opaque but still moist in thickest part; cut to test (about 6 minutes).

To serve, spoon polenta equally onto 4 dinner plates. Top each serving with a piece of fish; sprinkle with bell pepper and cilantro. Season to taste with salt; offer lime wedges to squeeze over fish to taste. Makes 4 servings.

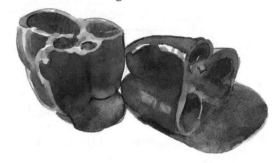

Poached Fish with Horseradish Sauce

Per serving:
208 calories (10% fat, 27% carbohydrates, 63% protein), 2 g
total fat (0.4 g saturated), 13 g carbohydrates, 32 g
protein, 89 mg cholesterol, 119 mg sodium

Preparation time: About 25 minutes

Cooking time: About 20 minutes

Tiny boiled potatoes and slivered green onions garnish a savory supper dish that's delicious prepared with any of a variety of fish. The simple sauce, based on the poaching liquid, gets a flavor boost from horseradish.

> 1½ **pounds boneless, skinless lingcod, halibut, rockfish, or sole fillets or steaks (fillets no thicker than 1 inch, steaks about 1 inch thick)**
>   **About ⅔ cup low-sodium chicken broth**
> 1 **tablespoon *each* cornstarch and prepared horseradish**
> 8 **to 12 hot boiled tiny potatoes (*each* about 1 inch in diameter)**
> 3 **green onions, cut into 2-inch lengths and slivered**

Rinse fish and pat dry; fold any thin fillets in half. Arrange fish in a shallow 8- or 9-inch baking dish. Pour ⅔ cup of the broth over fish. Cover and bake in a 400° oven until fish is just opaque but still moist in thickest part; cut to test (about 15 minutes). With a slotted spatula, lift fish to a warm platter; keep warm.

Drain cooking liquid from baking dish into a measuring cup; you should have about 1 cup. If necessary, boil to reduce to 1 cup or add more broth to make 1 cup. In a 1½- to 2-quart pan, smoothly blend cornstarch, horseradish, and cooking liquid. Bring to a boil over high heat, stirring.

To serve, spoon sauce evenly over fish. Arrange potatoes on platter around fish; sprinkle with onions. Makes 4 servings.

Whole Tilapia with Onion & Lemon

Per serving:
359 calories (22% fat, 40% carbohydrates, 38% protein),
10 g total fat (2 g saturated), 40 g carbohydrates, 38 g
protein, 82 mg cholesterol, 177 mg sodium

Preparation time: About 25 minutes

Baking time: About 20 minutes

Here's a delicious dinner for two: whole tilapia on a bed of onion and lemon slices. The mild fish has a clean, delicate flavor, much like that of petrale sole.

- 1¼ **pounds red onions, thinly sliced**
- 3 **tablespoons lemon juice**
- 1 **tablespoon minced fresh ginger**
- 1 **whole tilapia (about 1½ lbs.), dressed (gutted, with head and tail attached)**
- 1 **tablespoon extra-virgin olive oil**
- 2 **large lemons**
- 3 **tablespoons minced cilantro**
  Salt and pepper

In a large bowl, mix onions, lemon juice, and ginger. Set 1 or 2 onion slices aside, then spread remaining onion mixture in a 9- by 13-inch baking dish. Rinse fish, pat dry, and brush on both sides with oil; place on top of onion mixture.

Cut a ½-inch slice from both ends of each lemon. Stuff fish cavity with these lemon ends, reserved onion slices, and 1½ tablespoons of the cilantro. Thinly slice remainder of each lemon; tuck lemon slices around fish. Sprinkle remaining 1½ tablespoons cilantro over onion mixture and lemon slices. Bake in a 400° oven until fish is just opaque but still moist in thickest part; cut to test (about 20 minutes).

To serve, gently pull skin from fish; serve fish with onion-lemon mixture. Season to taste with salt and pepper. Makes 2 servings.

Grilled Tuna with Cherry Tomato Salsa

Per serving:
224 calories (29% fat, 21% carbohydrates, 50% protein), 7 g
total fat (2 g saturated), 12 g carbohydrates, 29 g protein,
43 mg cholesterol, 63 mg sodium

Preparation time: About 20 minutes

Grilling time: About 3 minutes

Fresh flavors and fast cooking characterize this easy-to-prepare entrée. If you prefer a less incendiary salsa, just eliminate one of the jalapeños.

- 1 **pound red or yellow cherry tomatoes (about 3 cups), coarsely chopped**
- ½ **cup lightly packed cilantro leaves, coarsely chopped**
- 2 **fresh jalapeño chiles, seeded and coarsely chopped**
- 1 **clove garlic, minced or pressed**
- 3 **green onions, thinly sliced**
- 5 **tablespoons lime juice**
- 1 **teaspoon olive oil**
- 4 **boneless, skinless tuna steaks (about 4 oz. each), ¾ to 1 inch thick**
- 2 **medium-size cucumbers (about 1 lb. *total*), thinly sliced**
  Freshly ground pepper

In a medium-size bowl, mix tomatoes, cilantro, chiles, garlic, onions, and 2 tablespoons of the lime juice. Cover and set aside.

Mix remaining 3 tablespoons lime juice with oil. Rinse tuna and pat dry; then brush both sides of each steak with oil mixture. Place tuna on a greased grill 4 to 6 inches above a solid bed of hot coals. Cook, turning once, until browned on outside but still pale pink in the center; cut to test (about 3 minutes).

Transfer tuna to a warm platter; surround with cucumber slices. Evenly top tuna with tomato salsa; season to taste with pepper. Makes 4 servings.

Pictured on facing page

Broiled Salmon & Asian-style Noodles

Per serving:
573 calories (28% fat, 42% carbohydrates, 30% protein),
18 g total fat (3 g saturated), 60 g carbohydrates, 44 g
protein, 94 mg cholesterol, 199 mg sodium

Preparation time: About 40 minutes

Chilling time: At least 30 minutes

Broiling time: About 4 minutes

For a memorable meal, a mixture of crisp salad greens and fresh herbs is topped first with cool pasta in vinaigrette, then with hot salmon fillets.

- 8 ounces dry capellini
- 5 tablespoons seasoned rice vinegar (or 5 tablespoons distilled white vinegar plus 2 tablespoons sugar)
- 5 tablespoons lime juice
- 5 teaspoons Oriental sesame oil
- ¼ teaspoon ground red pepper (cayenne)
- 2 teaspoons reduced-sodium soy sauce
- ½ cup thinly sliced green onions
- 4 thin boneless, skinless baby salmon fillets (about 6 oz. *each*)
- 5½ to 6 ounces mixed salad greens (about 8 cups), rinsed and crisped
- 1 cup *each* firmly packed cilantro leaves and fresh basil leaves, chopped

- 1 large cucumber (about 12 oz.), peeled, cut in half lengthwise, seeded, and thinly sliced crosswise

In a 5- to 6-quart pan, cook capellini in 3 quarts boiling water just until tender to bite (4 minutes); or cook according to package directions. Drain, rinse with cold water, and drain again. In a large bowl, mix 3 tablespoons each of the vinegar and lime juice, 4 teaspoons of the oil, red pepper, soy sauce, and onions. Stir in pasta, cover, and refrigerate until cool (at least 30 minutes) or for up to 2 hours.

Mix remaining 2 tablespoons lime juice with remaining 1 teaspoon oil. Rinse fish and pat dry; brush oil mixture over both sides of each fillet. Place fillets on rack of a 12- by 15-inch broiler pan. Broil about 4 inches below heat, turning once, until fish is just opaque but still moist in thickest part; cut to test (about 4 minutes).

In a large bowl, mix salad greens, cilantro, basil, and remaining 2 tablespoons vinegar. Divide mixture among 4 dinner plates; arrange pasta mixture and cucumber atop greens. Top each salad with a hot fish fillet. Makes 4 servings.

Pictured on front cover

Shrimp with Black Bean Sauce

Per serving:
181 calories (28% fat, 29% carbohydrates, 43% protein), 6 g
total fat (1 g saturated), 13 g carbohydrates, 20 g protein,
99 mg cholesterol, 579 mg sodium

Preparation time: About 30 minutes

Cooking time: About 10 minutes

This quick stir-fry is sure to win the approval of any time-conscious cook.

- 3 tablespoons fermented salted black beans, rinsed and drained
- 4 ounces lean ground pork
- 1 large red bell pepper (about 8 oz.), seeded and finely chopped
- 12 ounces mushrooms, thinly sliced
- 3 cloves garlic, minced or pressed
- 1 tablespoon minced fresh ginger
- 1 cup low-sodium chicken broth
- 2 tablespoons oyster sauce
- 1 tablespoon cornstarch

- 1 tablespoon salad oil
- 12 ounces shelled and deveined medium-size raw shrimp (40 to 45 per lb.)
- 6 green onions, thinly sliced
- 6 cups finely shredded napa cabbage (about 1½ lbs.)

In a large bowl, mix beans, pork, bell pepper, mushrooms, garlic, and ginger. In a small bowl, mix broth, oyster sauce, and cornstarch; set aside.

Heat oil in a wide nonstick frying pan over high heat. Add shrimp and cook, stirring, until opaque in center; cut to test (about 3 minutes). Remove from pan. Add pork mixture to pan and cook, stirring, until meat is lightly browned (about 5 minutes). Add broth mixture; bring to a boil, stirring. Mix in shrimp and onions. Arrange cabbage on a platter; top with shrimp mixture. Makes 6 servings.

Broiled Salmon & Asian-style Noodles (recipe on facing page) contrasts
hot-from-the-broiler baby salmon fillets with crisp greens and a cool
capellini salad. Serve this unusual and elegant entrée with
Japanese rice crackers and frosty iced tea.

Seafood & Spinach Stew

Per serving:
*220 **calories** (15% fat, 38% carbohydrates, 47% protein), 4 g **total fat** (1 g saturated), 21 g **carbohydrates**, 26 g **protein**, 88 mg **cholesterol**, 169 mg **sodium***

Preparation time: About 30 minutes

Cooking time: About 30 minutes

Cut down on cleanup with this one-pot meal. Halibut, shrimp, potatoes, and tomatoes simmer together in a lemon-scented broth; slivered spinach makes a pretty garnish.

- **4 cups low-sodium chicken broth**
- **1 tablespoon shredded lemon peel**
- **¼ cup minced fresh basil or 2 tablespoons dry basil**
- **1 tablespoon minced fresh thyme or 1 teaspoon dry thyme**
- **1 pound small red thin-skinned potatoes (*each* about 1½ inches in diameter), scrubbed**
- **8 ounces spinach, stems removed, leaves rinsed and drained**
- **12 ounces firm-textured, white-fleshed fish such as halibut, sea bass, or shark, cut into 1½-inch chunks**
- **12 ounces large raw shrimp (31 to 35 per lb.), shelled and deveined**
- **1 pound pear-shaped (Roma-type) tomatoes, coarsely chopped**

In a 4- to 5-quart pan, combine broth, lemon peel, basil, thyme, and potatoes. Bring to a boil over high heat; reduce heat, cover, and boil gently until potatoes are just tender when pierced (about 20 minutes).

Meanwhile, cut spinach leaves lengthwise into slivers about ⅛ inch wide; set aside.

Return broth to a rolling boil over high heat; add fish. Reduce heat to low, cover, and simmer for 2 minutes. Stir in shrimp, tomatoes, and half the spinach. Cover; continue to simmer until fish is just opaque but still moist in thickest part and shrimp are opaque in center; cut to test (about 3 minutes).

To serve, divide stew among 6 wide, shallow bowls. Garnish with remaining spinach. Makes 6 servings.

Cajun Scallops & Brown Rice

Per serving:
*350 **calories** (20% fat, 50% carbohydrates, 30% protein), 8 g **total fat** (2 g saturated), 43 g **carbohydrates**, 26 g **protein**, 44 mg **cholesterol**, 226 mg **sodium***

Preparation time: About 10 minutes

Cooking time: About 45 minutes

Warm up appetites with this bay scallop dish. It's spicy—but the light cream sauce helps keep the heat under control. Serve on a bed of brown rice, with a medley of your favorite seasonal vegetables on the side.

- **4½ cups low-sodium chicken broth**
- **1½ cups long-grain brown rice**
- **1½ pounds bay scallops**
- **1 teaspoon paprika**
- **½ teaspoon ground white pepper**
- **¼ teaspoon ground allspice**
- **2 teaspoons salad oil**
- **1½ tablespoons cornstarch mixed with ⅓ cup cold water**
- **½ cup reduced-fat sour cream**
- **Parsley sprigs**

In a 3- to 4-quart pan, bring 3½ cups of the broth to a boil over high heat. Add rice; reduce heat, cover, and simmer until rice is tender to bite (about 45 minutes).

About 10 minutes before rice is done, rinse and drain scallops; then mix with paprika, white pepper, and allspice. Heat oil in a wide nonstick frying pan over high heat. Add scallops and cook, stirring, until opaque in center; cut to test (about 3 minutes). With a slotted spoon, transfer scallops to a bowl.

Bring pan juices to a boil over high heat; boil until reduced to ¼ cup. Add remaining 1 cup broth and return to a boil. Stir in cornstarch mixture; bring to a boil, stirring. Stir in sour cream and scallops. Serve over brown rice; garnish with parsley sprigs. Makes 6 servings.

Vermicelli with Sake Clam Sauce

Per serving:
*411 **calories** (5% fat, 69% carbohydrates, 26% protein), 2 g **total fat** (0.3 g saturated), 59 g **carbohydrates**, 22 g **protein**, 32 mg **cholesterol**, 173 mg **sodium***

Preparation time: About 10 minutes

Cooking time: About 10 minutes

Robust flavor and time-saving preparation make this dish a suppertime standout. Tender pasta in a sauce of sake and chopped clams is tossed with cheese, hot red pepper, and parsley.

- 2 cans (about 6½ oz. *each*) chopped clams
- ¾ cup finely chopped onion
- 2 cloves garlic, minced or pressed
- 1 cup sake or dry vermouth
- 2 tablespoons drained capers
- 10 ounces dry vermicelli or linguine, cooked and drained (keep hot)
- ¼ cup finely chopped parsley
- ¼ cup freshly grated Parmesan cheese (optional)
  About ⅛ teaspoon crushed red pepper flakes

Drain clams, reserving ½ cup of the juice. In a wide frying pan, combine reserved clam juice, onion, garlic, and ¼ cup of the sake. Cook over high heat, stirring, until mixture is reduced by about three-fourths. Add remaining ¾ cup sake, clams, and capers; reduce heat and simmer for about 3 minutes.

Pour hot pasta into a warm wide bowl; add clam sauce. Lift and mix with 2 forks until almost all liquid is absorbed. Top with parsley, cheese (if desired), and red pepper flakes; mix again. Makes 4 servings.

Crab Lasagne with Roasted Fennel

Per serving:
*417 **calories** (28% fat, 43% carbohydrates, 29% protein), 13 g **total fat** (7 g saturated), 43 g **carbohydrates**, 30 g **protein**, 96 mg **cholesterol**, 594 mg **sodium***

Preparation time: About 2 hours

Baking & broiling time: About 14 minutes

A little crab goes a long way when it's mixed with vegetables in a creamy cheese sauce, then layered with lasagne noodles.

- 2¼ pounds fennel
- 2 large onions, thinly sliced
- 12 ounces mushrooms, sliced
- 2 cups low-sodium chicken broth
- 2 cups nonfat or lowfat milk
- ¼ cup dry sherry
- ¼ cup cornstarch mixed with ⅓ cup cold water
- 2 cups (about 8 oz.) shredded fontina cheese
- 8 ounces dry lasagne noodles, cooked, drained, and blotted dry
- ¾ to 1 pound cooked crabmeat

Cut feathery tops from fennel; set aside. Cut root ends and any bruised spots from fennel heads; then thinly slice fennel crosswise. In a 12- by 14-inch roasting pan, mix sliced fennel, onions, and mushrooms. Bake, uncovered, in a 475° oven, stirring occasionally, until browned bits form on pan bottom (about 45 minutes).

Add ½ cup of the broth to pan; stir to loosen browned bits. Continue to bake until browned bits form in pan again (about 20 more minutes). Add ½ cup more broth and stir to loosen browned bits; continue to bake until vegetables are well browned (about 20 more minutes). Add ½ cup more broth, stir to loosen browned bits, and keep warm.

Mince enough of the reserved fennel tops to make ¼ cup. In a wide frying pan, combine minced fennel, remaining ½ cup broth, milk, and sherry. Bring to a boil. Stir in cornstarch mixture; bring to a boil, stirring. Remove from heat. Add 1 cup of the cheese, stir until smooth, and keep hot.

Cover bottom of a 9- by 13-inch baking dish with a third of the lasagne noodles. Spread with all the vegetables and half the sauce. Cover with half the remaining noodles; top with all the crab and all but ½ cup of the remaining sauce. Cover with remaining noodles; top with remaining ½ cup sauce and remaining 1 cup cheese.

Bake in a 450° oven until sauce is bubbly (about 10 minutes); then broil 4 to 6 inches below heat until cheese is browned (about 4 minutes). Let stand for 5 minutes before serving. Makes 6 to 8 servings.

Mix steaming-hot pasta with a tempting sauce of Swiss chard, lentils, and Neufchâtel cheese to create hearty Linguine with Lentils (recipe on page 60). Serve with juicy, basil-scented tomato slices, a loaf of whole-grain bread, and a jug of fruity red wine for a filling vegetarian meal.

Vegetarian Entrées

Versatile vegetables, changing colorfully with the seasons,

bring balance and variety to lowfat meals. But don't think

of them solely as accompaniments; as this chapter shows,

vegetables make superb main dishes. Because the protein in

vegetables is incomplete, our recipes complement fresh

produce with pasta, grains, and legumes for satisfying,

fiber-rich entrées. Dairy products and eggs will complete

vegetable proteins, too, but be sure to add these foods in

moderation. Select nonfat milk products or those with only

one or two percent milk fat; to avoid the fat in egg yolks,

replace whole eggs with egg whites when possible.

Baked Shells & Fontina

Per serving:
396 **calories** (29% fat, 50% carbohydrates, 21% protein), 13 g **total fat** (7 g saturated), 50 g **carbohydrates**, 21 g **protein**, 37 mg **cholesterol**, 744 mg **sodium**

Preparation time: About 45 minutes

Baking time: About 35 minutes

Broccoli, carrots, and peas brighten up this contemporary version of macaroni and cheese.

  1 tablespoon margarine
  2 vegetable bouillon cubes dissolved in 2 cups boiling water
  ¼ cup finely chopped shallots
  ¼ cup all-purpose flour
  1½ cups nonfat milk
  1½ cups (about 6 oz.) shredded fontina cheese
  ½ teaspoon ground nutmeg
  8 ounces dry medium-size shell-shaped pasta
  3 medium-size carrots (about 9 oz. *total*), cut into thin slanting slices
  3 cups broccoli flowerets (about 12 oz.)
  1 package (about 10 oz.) frozen tiny peas
  ¼ cup grated Parmesan cheese

In a 2-quart pan, combine margarine and ¼ cup of the bouillon. Heat over medium heat until margarine is melted; add shallots and cook, stirring occasionally, until soft but not browned (about 5 minutes). Add flour and cook, stirring, until bubbly. Remove pan from heat and gradually stir in milk and remaining 1¾ cups bouillon; return to medium heat and bring to a boil, stirring (about 8 minutes). Remove from heat, add fontina cheese and nutmeg, and stir until cheese is melted.

In a 5- to 6-quart pan, cook pasta in 3 quarts boiling water just until almost tender to bite (about 8 minutes); or cook for a little less than time specified in package directions. After pasta has cooked for 5 minutes, add carrots to pan; after 3 more minutes, add broccoli. Drain pasta and vegetables well; pour into a large bowl. Mix in cheese sauce and peas.

Spread pasta mixture in a greased 2- to 2½-quart baking dish; sprinkle with Parmesan cheese. Bake, uncovered, in a 400° oven until golden brown on top (about 35 minutes). Makes 6 servings.

Pictured on page 58

Linguine with Lentils

Per serving:
462 **calories** (24% fat, 58% carbohydrates, 18% protein), 13 g **total fat** (5 g saturated), 67 g **carbohydrates**, 21 g **protein**, 22 mg **cholesterol**, 730 mg **sodium**

Preparation time: About 15 minutes

Cooking time: About 55 minutes

Lentils and Swiss chard, flavored in a spicy broth, combine with linguine and creamy Neufchâtel cheese for a satisfying main dish.

  3 vegetable bouillon cubes dissolved in 3 cups boiling water
  1 cup lentils, rinsed and drained
  1 teaspoon cumin seeds
  1 pound Swiss chard
  2 tablespoons olive oil
  1 large onion, chopped
  2 cloves garlic, minced or pressed
  ½ teaspoon crushed red pepper flakes
  12 ounces dry linguine
  6 ounces Neufchâtel cheese, diced
    Salt and pepper

In a 5- to 6-quart pan, bring 2 cups of the bouillon to a boil over high heat. Add lentils and cumin seeds. Reduce heat, cover, and simmer until lentils are tender to bite (about 30 minutes). Drain, if necessary; then pour into a bowl.

Rinse chard well. Cut off and discard coarse stem ends; cut stems and leaves crosswise into ¼-inch-wide strips (keep stems and leaves separate).

To lentil cooking pan, add oil, chard stems, onion, garlic, and red pepper flakes. Cook over medium heat, stirring often, until onion is lightly browned (about 15 minutes). Add chard leaves; cook, stirring, until limp (about 3 minutes). Add lentils and remaining 1 cup bouillon; cook, uncovered, until hot (about 3 minutes).

Meanwhile, in another 5- to 6-quart pan, cook linguine in 3 quarts boiling water just until tender to bite (about 7 minutes). Drain pasta and pour into a wide bowl. Add lentil mixture and cheese; mix lightly to blend. Season to taste with salt and pepper. Makes 6 servings.

Curried Bean & Barley Stew

Per serving:
216 calories (4% fat, 76% carbohydrates, 20% protein), 1 g total fat (0.1 g saturated), 43 g carbohydrates, 11 g protein, 0 mg cholesterol, 1,204 mg sodium

Preparation time: About 15 minutes

Standing time: 1 hour

Cooking time: About 50 minutes

This hearty, curry-seasoned stew is bound to become one of your favorite one-pot meals. Three kinds of legumes—kidney beans, pinto beans, and black-eyed peas—combine with barley and vegetables in an easy-to-prepare entrée for a chilly night.

- ¼ cup *each* dried kidney beans, pinto beans, and black-eyed peas
- ¼ cup pearl barley, rinsed and drained
- 5 vegetable bouillon cubes dissolved in 5 cups boiling water
- 1 large onion, chopped
- 1 cup chopped celery
- 2 cups thinly sliced carrots
- 2 teaspoons curry powder
- 1 teaspoon ground turmeric
- 1½ tablespoons cider vinegar

Sort through kidney beans, pinto beans, and black-eyed peas; discard any debris. Rinse and drain peas and beans; place in a 4- to 5-quart pan and stir in barley. Add enough water to cover by 1 inch. Bring to a boil over high heat; then boil, uncovered, for 2 minutes. Remove from heat, cover, and let stand for 1 hour. Drain well and return to pan.

To pan, add bouillon, onion, celery, carrots, curry powder, and turmeric. Bring to a boil over high heat; reduce heat to medium, cover, and simmer until beans are tender to bite (about 45 minutes). Stir in vinegar and simmer for 5 more minutes. Makes 4 servings.

Alsatian Gratin of Roots

Per serving:
324 calories (8% fat, 78% carbohydrates, 14% protein), 3 g total fat (1 g saturated), 63 g carbohydrates, 11 g protein, 6 mg cholesterol, 584 mg sodium

Preparation time: About 1¾ hours

Baking & broiling time: About 1½ hours

Enjoy the sweet and earthy flavors of winter root vegetables in this cold-weather casserole. Serve it bubbling hot, perhaps with a hearty salad of cooked lentils in an herb vinaigrette.

- 3 large onions, finely chopped
- 4 large carrots (about 1 lb. *total*), finely chopped
- 3 vegetable bouillon cubes dissolved in 3 cups boiling water
- 3 pounds thin-skinned potatoes
- 1 pound rutabagas
- ½ cup minced parsley
  About ½ teaspoon freshly grated nutmeg
- ¾ cup shredded reduced-fat Jarlsberg cheese
  Salt and pepper

In a 5- to 6-quart pan, combine onions, carrots, and ½ cup of the bouillon. Cook over high heat, stirring occasionally, until liquid evaporates and vegetables begin to brown. To deglaze, add 2 to 3 tablespoons more bouillon and stir to loosen browned bits. Then cook, stirring occasionally, until liquid evaporates and vegetables begin to brown again. Repeat deglazing step, using about 2 tablespoons of liquid each time, until vegetables are richly browned; use bouillon the first 2 or 3 times, then use water if more deglazing is needed. When deglazing the last time, do not cook vegetables dry.

Peel and very thinly slice potatoes and rutabagas. In a shallow 4-quart casserole, arrange layers of potatoes, rutabagas, onion-carrot mixture, parsley, and light sprinklings of nutmeg; start and finish with a layer of potatoes. Pour remaining bouillon (about 2 cups) into casserole; cover tightly with a piece of lightly oiled foil, oiled side down.

Bake in a 425° oven until vegetables in center of casserole are very tender when pierced (about 1½ hours). Then uncover, sprinkle with cheese, dust lightly with nutmeg, and broil about 8 inches below heat until cheese is bubbly and lightly browned (about 5 minutes). Season to taste with salt and pepper. Makes 6 servings.

Corn & Asparagus Risotto

Per serving:
272 *calories* (10% fat, 74% carbohydrates, 16% protein), 3 g *total fat* (1 g saturated), 53 g *carbohydrates*, 11 g *protein*, 6 mg *cholesterol*, 843 mg *sodium*

Preparation time: About 15 minutes

Cooking time: About 35 minutes

Studded with asparagus tips and corn kernels, this creamy, sage-seasoned risotto makes a filling main dish. Serve it with crusty bread and mixed greens sprinkled with balsamic vinegar.

- 1 **large onion, finely chopped**
- 4 **vegetable bouillon cubes dissolved in 4 cups boiling water**
- 1 **cup short-grain white rice (such as arborio or pearl)**
- 1 **can (about 17 oz.) no-salt-added whole-kernel corn, drained**
- 1 **pound asparagus tips, cut diagonally into 2-inch pieces**
- 1 **teaspoon dry sage**
- ¼ **cup *each* grated Parmesan cheese and shredded part-skim mozzarella cheese**

In a wide frying pan (preferably nonstick), combine onion and ½ cup of the bouillon. Cook over high heat, stirring occasionally, until almost all liquid has evaporated and onion is soft but not browned. Add rice; cook, stirring, until opaque and milky looking (about 2 minutes). Stir in corn.

Add remaining 3½ cups bouillon and bring to a boil, stirring often. Reduce heat and simmer, uncovered, stirring occasionally, for 15 minutes. Add asparagus; continue to cook, uncovered, until rice and asparagus are just tender to bite and almost all liquid has been absorbed (about 5 more minutes). Remove mixture from heat and gently stir in sage, Parmesan cheese, and mozzarella cheese; let stand until cheese is melted (about 2 minutes). Makes 4 to 6 servings.

Pictured on facing page

Ratatouille-topped Baked Potatoes

Per serving:
290 *calories* (10% fat, 80% carbohydrates, 10% protein), 3 g *total fat* (0.4 g saturated), 60 g *carbohydrates*, 8 g *protein*, 0 mg *cholesterol*, 35 mg *sodium*

Preparation time: About 25 minutes

Baking time: About 1½ hours

Fluffy baked potatoes are filled to overflowing with a medley of herb-seasoned garden vegetables— eggplant, zucchini, crookneck squash, bell pepper, and tomatoes.

- 1 **medium-size eggplant (about 1 lb.), unpeeled, cut into ½- by 2-inch sticks**
- 8 **ounces *each* zucchini and crookneck squash, cut into ½-inch-thick slices**
- 1½ **pounds pear-shaped (Roma-type) tomatoes, quartered**
- 1 ***each* large red and yellow bell pepper (about 1 lb. *total*), thinly sliced**
- 1 **large onion, chopped**
- 3 **garlic cloves, minced or pressed**
- 1 **dry bay leaf**
- ½ **teaspoon *each* dry thyme and dry rosemary**
- 1 **tablespoon olive oil**
- 6 **large red thin-skinned potatoes (about 8 oz. *each*), scrubbed**

  Freshly ground pepper

In a 3- to 4-quart baking dish, mix eggplant, zucchini, crookneck squash, tomatoes, bell peppers, onion, garlic, bay leaf, thyme, rosemary, and oil. Cover and bake in a 400° oven for 1 hour. Uncover and continue to bake, stirring once or twice, until eggplant is very soft when pressed and only a thin layer of liquid remains in bottom of dish (about 30 more minutes).

After eggplant mixture has baked for 30 minutes, pierce each unpeeled potato in several places with a fork; place potatoes on a baking sheet and bake until tender throughout when pierced (about 1 hour).

To serve, make a deep cut lengthwise down center of each potato; then make a second cut across center. Grasp each potato between cuts; press firmly to split potato wide open. Spoon eggplant mixture equally into potatoes; season to taste with pepper. Makes 6 servings.

*Crowned with a garden of vegetable delights, herbed
Ratatouille-topped Baked Potatoes (recipe on facing page) look and
taste delicious. Round out an appealing supper with crisp corn
muffins and steamed fresh green beans.*

Sweet Potato Pizza

Per serving:
333 **calories** *(24% fat, 65% carbohydrates, 11% protein), 9 g*
total fat *(3 g saturated), 56 g* **carbohydrates**, *10 g* **protein**,
116 mg **cholesterol**, *166 mg* **sodium**

Preparation time: About 30 minutes

Baking time: About 45 minutes

This unusual pizza is really a crisp sweet potato pancake, richly seasoned with onions, pepper, and sage. Add toppings of applesauce and cool sour cream to taste.

- 1 tablespoon olive oil
- 2¾ cups fine sourdough bread crumbs (about 5 sandwich-size slices)
- 4 cloves garlic, minced or pressed
- 4 large eggs
- 2 large egg whites
- 2 teaspoons dry sage
- ½ teaspoon pepper
- 1½ pounds sweet potatoes
- 2 large onions, finely chopped
- 1 cup reduced-fat sour cream
- 4 cups applesauce

Heat oil in a wide frying pan (preferably nonstick) over medium-high heat; add crumbs and garlic. Cook, stirring, until crumbs are crisp (about 8 minutes). Remove from heat and set aside.

In a large bowl, beat eggs, egg whites, sage, and pepper until well blended. Peel and shred potatoes; add potatoes, onions, and crumbs to egg mixture and mix well. Divide potato mixture equally between 2 well-greased, floured 12-inch nonstick pizza pans; spread evenly (be sure edges and middle are equally thick, or edges will burn).

Bake in a 400° oven until potato cake is crisp and browned (about 45 minutes). With a spatula, loosen cake from pan; cut into wedges. Add sour cream and applesauce to taste. Makes 8 servings.

Picadillo-stuffed Peppers

Per serving:
308 **calories** *(19% fat, 69% carbohydrates, 12% protein), 7 g*
total fat *(1 g saturated), 55 g* **carbohydrates**, *9 g* **protein**,
1 mg **cholesterol**, *171 mg* **sodium**

Preparation time: About 30 minutes

Baking time: About 45 minutes

Brown rice and black beans in a savory-sweet, raisin-dotted tomato sauce make a delicious filling for big, bright bell peppers.

- 6 medium-size yellow bell peppers (about 2¼ lbs. *total*)
- 1 tablespoon olive oil
- 2 cloves garlic, minced or pressed
- 1 large can (about 15 oz.) no-salt-added tomato sauce
- ¼ cup dry white wine
- 2 tablespoons cider vinegar
- 1½ teaspoons ground cinnamon
- 1 teaspoon dry oregano
- ½ cup raisins
- 3 cups cooked brown rice
- 1 can (about 15 oz.) black beans, drained and rinsed
- ¼ cup sliced almonds
- 2 tablespoons grated Parmesan cheese

Cut off stem ends of peppers and remove seeds. Trim bases slightly so peppers will stand upright. In a 6- to 8-quart pan, bring 3 to 4 quarts water to a boil over high heat. Add peppers; cook for 2 minutes. Using tongs, carefully lift peppers from pan and plunge into cold water to cool; drain.

Heat oil in a wide frying pan (preferably nonstick) over medium-high heat. Add garlic; cook, stirring, just until soft (about 2 minutes). Add 1 cup of the tomato sauce, wine, vinegar, cinnamon, oregano, and raisins; cook, stirring occasionally, for 15 minutes. Stir in rice, beans, and almonds.

Fill peppers equally with rice mixture; set upright in a shallow 1½-quart baking pan. Pour remaining tomato sauce into pan around peppers. Cover and bake in a 375° oven for 30 minutes. Uncover; top peppers evenly with cheese and continue to bake until cheese is golden brown (about 15 more minutes). Makes 6 servings.

Spaghetti Squash with Fresh Tomato Sauce

Per serving:
252 calories (21% fat, 63% carbohydrates, 16% protein), 5 g total fat (2 g saturated), 34 g carbohydrates, 9 g protein, 8 mg cholesterol, 453 mg sodium

Preparation time: About 15 minutes

Baking time: About 1 ¼ hours

Tender-crisp spaghetti squash takes the place of pasta in this hearty main dish. Top the mild-flavored strands with a white wine sauce loaded with fresh tomatoes, minced onion, and peas.

- 1 medium-size spaghetti squash (about 4 lbs.)
- 1 large onion, chopped
- 1 clove garlic, minced or pressed
- 1 vegetable bouillon cube dissolved in 1 cup boiling water
- 12 ounces pear-shaped (Roma-type) tomatoes, chopped
- 1 teaspoon *each* dry basil and dry oregano
- 2 tablespoons tomato paste
- 1½ cups dry white wine
- 1 package (about 10 oz.) frozen peas, thawed
- ½ cup shredded provolone cheese

Pierce shell of spaghetti squash in several places. Set squash on a foil-lined baking sheet and bake in a 350° oven for 45 minutes. Turn squash over; continue to bake until shell gives when pressed (about 25 more minutes). Cut squash in half horizontally. Discard seeds; pull strands free with a fork, leaving them in squash halves.

While squash is baking, in a wide frying pan (preferably nonstick), combine onion, garlic, and ½ cup of the bouillon. Cook over high heat, stirring occasionally, until almost all liquid has evaporated and onion is soft but not browned. Add remaining ½ cup bouillon, tomatoes, basil, oregano, tomato paste, and wine; bring to a boil. Reduce heat to medium-high and boil gently, stirring occasionally, until almost all liquid has evaporated (about 10 more minutes). Stir in peas.

Scoop strands from squash halves and spread in a greased shallow 2- to 2½-quart casserole; cover with sauce and sprinkle with cheese. Return to oven and bake just until cheese is melted (about 3 minutes). Makes 4 to 6 servings.

Zucchini Burgers

Per serving:
276 calories (25% fat, 57% carbohydrates, 18% protein), 8 g total fat (2 g saturated), 40 g carbohydrates, 13 g protein, 74 mg cholesterol, 481 mg sodium

Preparation time: About 30 minutes

Cooking time: About 12 minutes

Here's a new way to enjoy the summer's zucchini crop. Shred the squash and stir in chopped onion and Parmesan cheese; then make crisp, gold-green cakes to serve on toasted onion bagels.

- 1½ pounds zucchini, coarsely shredded
- 2 tablespoons margarine
- 1 large onion, finely chopped
- ¼ cup fine dry bread crumbs
- 2 large eggs, lightly beaten
- ¼ cup grated Parmesan cheese
- 6 onion bagels, split and toasted
  Tartar sauce or catsup

Drain zucchini in a colander for 30 minutes; then squeeze to remove moisture.

While zucchini is draining, melt 2 teaspoons of the margarine in a wide nonstick frying pan over medium heat. Add onion; stir often until lightly browned (about 10 minutes). Scrape into a bowl.

Mix drained zucchini, crumbs, eggs, and cheese with onion in bowl. In frying pan, melt remaining 4 teaspoons margarine over medium-high heat. Ladle three ¼-cup mounds of zucchini mixture into pan, spreading each to make a 3-inch-wide cake. Cook until cakes are lightly browned on bottom (about 3 minutes). With a wide spatula, turn cakes over; continue to cook until browned on other side (about 3 more minutes). Remove from pan and keep warm. Repeat to cook remaining zucchini mixture, making 3 more cakes.

To serve, place zucchini cakes on bagels; add tartar sauce to taste. Makes 6 servings.

For a light and stylish dinner, accompany skewers of plump
broiled shrimp with a pair of bright vegetable dishes: cool, Asian-seasoned
Sherried Green Beans & Peas and hot, orange-accented Honey Carrots
with Currants (recipes on page 68).

Side Dishes

Tender-crisp vegetables, tart-sweet fruits, savory legumes, nutty-flavored whole grains—all deliver welcome diversity to lowfat menus. Simply prepared meats, chicken, and fish perk up when they share the plate with such accompaniments as cool and zesty Cauliflower with Toasted Mustard Seeds or sophisticated, sherry-spiked Barley & Brown Rice Pilaf. Besides pleasing flavors and cheerful appearance, our sparkling side dishes also bring necessary vitamins, minerals, and complex carbohydrates to your meals.

Pictured on page 66

Sherried Green Beans & Peas

Preparation time: About 15 minutes

Cooking time: About 7 minutes

Tender-crisp green beans and tiny peas, cooled and tossed with a simple sherry-soy sauce, make a refreshing side dish you can easily prepare ahead. Add the garnish—a sprinkling of diced bell pepper—just before serving.

> 1½ **pounds tender green beans, ends and strings removed**
> 1 **package (about 10 oz.) frozen tiny peas**
> 2 **teaspoons cornstarch**
> 1 **tablespoon minced fresh ginger**
> 2 **tablespoons reduced-sodium soy sauce**
> ¼ **cup dry sherry**
> ½ **cup water**
> 1 **tablespoon Oriental sesame oil**
> ¼ **cup finely diced red bell pepper**

In a 4- to 5-quart pan, bring about 8 cups water to a boil over high heat. Add beans and cook, uncov-

Per serving:
70 **calories** *(22% fat, 61% carbohydrates, 17% protein), 2 g* **total fat** *(0.2 g saturated), 10 g* **carbohydrates**, *3 g* **protein**, *0 mg* **cholesterol**, *181 mg* **sodium**

ered, just until tender to bite (about 6 minutes). Stir in peas, then drain vegetables well. Immerse in ice water until cool; drain and pour into a wide serving bowl or rimmed platter.

In same pan, blend cornstarch, ginger, soy sauce, sherry, and the ½ cup water; bring to a boil over high heat, stirring. Let cool; stir in oil. (At this point, you may cover and refrigerate vegetables and sherry sauce separately until next day.)

To serve, pour sherry sauce over vegetables; mix gently. Garnish with bell pepper. Makes 8 to 10 servings.

Pictured on page 66

Honey Carrots with Currants

Preparation time: About 15 minutes

Cooking time: About 15 minutes

Thin carrot sticks are cooked with honey and lemon just until tender, then dressed up with a tangy-sweet topping of orange juice, chutney, and currants. Offer the dish warm; or prepare both carrots and topping ahead, then serve cold.

> 1½ **cups water**
> 6 **large carrots (about 1½ lbs. *total*), cut into ⅛-inch-thick, 3- to 4-inch-long sticks**
> 2 **tablespoons *each* honey and lemon juice**
> ¼ **cup dried currants**
> ¼ **cup Major Grey's chutney, minced**
> ¼ **cup orange juice**
> **Salt**
> **Finely slivered orange peel**

Per serving:
108 **calories** *(2% fat, 94% carbohydrates, 4% protein), 0.2 g* **total fat** *(0 g saturated), 27 g* **carbohydrates**, *1 g* **protein**, *0 mg* **cholesterol**, *137 mg* **sodium**

In a 4- to 5-quart pan, bring water to a boil over high heat; add carrots, honey, and lemon juice. Cook, stirring often, until carrots are barely tender to bite (about 3 minutes). Drain carrots, reserving liquid; place carrots in a rimmed serving dish and keep warm.

Return cooking liquid to pan; bring to a boil over high heat. Boil, uncovered, until reduced to about ¼ cup (about 10 minutes). Add currants; stir until liquid begins to caramelize and currants look puffy. Stir in chutney. (At this point, you may let carrots and currant topping cool, then cover and refrigerate separately until next day.)

To serve, mix orange juice into currant topping; then spoon topping over carrots. Season to taste with salt; sprinkle with orange peel. Makes 6 to 8 servings.

Cauliflower with Toasted Mustard Seeds

Per serving:
139 calories (18% fat, 53% carbohydrates, 29% protein), 3 g total fat (0.3 g saturated), 20 g carbohydrates, 11 g protein, 2 mg cholesterol, 90 mg sodium

Preparation time: About 15 minutes

Cooking time: About 13 minutes

When the weather turns hot, cooling side dishes like this one are especially welcome. Tender cauliflowerets, cloaked in a mint- and mustard-flavored yogurt sauce and presented on crisp lettuce, are a perfect partner for smoked turkey or cold sliced meats.

 3 tablespoons mustard seeds
 1 large head cauliflower (about 2 lbs.), stem and leaves trimmed
 1½ cups plain nonfat or lowfat yogurt
 ¼ cup minced fresh mint or 2 tablespoons dry mint
 2 teaspoons sugar
 1 teaspoon ground cumin
 1 small head romaine lettuce (about 8 oz.), separated into leaves, rinsed, and crisped
 Mint sprigs (optional)

Toast mustard seeds in a small frying pan over medium heat until seeds turn gray (about 5 minutes), shaking pan often. Set aside.

Cut cauliflower into bite-size flowerets, then place on a rack over 1 inch of boiling water in a 5- to 6-quart pan; cover and steam until tender when pierced (about 8 minutes). Immerse cauliflower in ice water until cool, then drain well on paper towels.

In a large bowl, mix yogurt, minced mint, sugar, cumin, and 2 tablespoons of the mustard seeds. Add cauliflower and mix gently to coat well. (At this point, you may cover and refrigerate for up to 4 hours.)

To serve, arrange lettuce leaves on a platter. Spoon cauliflower mixture into lettuce; sprinkle with remaining 1 tablespoon mustard seeds. Garnish with mint sprigs, if desired. Makes 4 servings.

Chard-Rice Packets

Per serving:
113 calories (14% fat, 69% carbohydrates, 17% protein), 2 g total fat (0 g saturated), 20 g carbohydrates, 5 g protein, 5 mg cholesterol, 538 mg sodium

Preparation time: About 30 minutes

Baking time: About 20 minutes

Delight your family or friends with appealing vegetable "surprise packages": Swiss chard leaves wrapped around a filling of chiles, cilantro, cheese, and rice.

 8 large Swiss chard leaves (1 to 1½ lbs. *total*; green parts should be about 6 by 8 inches)
 2 cups cooked white rice
 1 large can (about 7 oz.) diced green chiles
 2 ounces reduced-fat jack cheese, diced
 3 tablespoons chopped cilantro
 ½ teaspoon pepper
 1 can (about 14½ oz.) Mexican-style stewed tomatoes

In a 5- to 6-quart pan, bring about 3 quarts water to a boil. Rinse and drain chard leaves, then cut off stems; plunge stems into boiling water and cook until tender when pierced (about 4 minutes). Lift from water and drain. Add leaves to water and cook until limp (about 1 minute). Drain.

Coarsely chop chard stems, place in a large bowl, and mix in rice, chiles, cheese, cilantro, and pepper. Place an eighth of the rice mixture in center of each chard leaf. Wrap sides and ends of leaves around filling to enclose. Place packets, seam sides down, in a shallow 3-quart baking dish. Cut up tomatoes, then pour tomatoes and their liquid around packets.

Cover and bake in a 400° oven until filling is hot in center; cut to test (about 20 minutes). To serve, lift packets to a warm platter or plates; spoon tomatoes over packets. Makes 8 servings.

Pictured on facing page

Cranberry-Tomato Relish in Lemon Shells

Per serving:
133 **calories** *(2% fat, 95% carbohydrates, 3% protein), 0.3 g*
total fat *(0 g saturated), 34 g* **carbohydrates**, *1 g* **protein**,
0 mg **cholesterol**, *145 mg* **sodium**

Preparation time: About 20 minutes

Cooking time: About 50 minutes

You'll begin a new tradition when you serve our sweet-tart cranberry-tomato relish with the family's favorite holiday roast. For an especially pretty presentation, spoon the relish into decoratively cut lemon halves.

- **4 or 5 lemons** (*each* **about 3½ inches long); or ½ cup fresh lemon juice**
- **1 large can (about 28 oz.) tomatoes**
- **1 large onion, finely chopped**
- **1 cup sugar**
- **2 tablespoons minced fresh ginger**
- **1 package (about 12 oz.) fresh or frozen cranberries**

If using lemons for serving containers, cut them in half crosswise (cut decorative zigzag edges, if desired). Squeeze out juice and set aside; then scoop out and discard pulp and membranes from lemon shells. Trim a thin slice from base of each shell so it will sit steadily upright. Wrap shells in paper towels, enclose in a plastic bag, and refrigerate; use within 2 days.

Measure ½ cup of the lemon juice and pour into a wide frying pan or 5-quart pan. Cut up tomatoes; add tomatoes and their liquid to pan. Then add onion, sugar, and ginger. Bring to a boil over medium-high heat; boil, uncovered, stirring often, for 20 minutes.

Add cranberries and continue to cook, uncovered, stirring often, until relish is reduced to about 3½ cups (about 30 more minutes). As relish thickens, watch carefully and stir more often to prevent scorching. Let cool. If made ahead, cover and refrigerate for up to 3 weeks.

To serve, divide relish equally among lemon shells (if using); or spoon into small (about ⅓-cup size) cups or bowls. Arrange on a large platter around an entrée. Makes 8 to 10 servings.

Pictured on facing page

Parsnips & Pears in Ginger Milk

Per serving:
146 **calories** *(6% fat, 82% carbohydrates, 12% protein), 1 g*
total fat *(0.2 g saturated), 32 g* **carbohydrates**, *5 g* **protein**,
1 mg **cholesterol**, *126 mg* **sodium**

Preparation time: About 30 minutes

Baking time: About 45 minutes

Warm up a winter meal with this hearty and easily assembled casserole. Layers of thinly sliced onion, parsnips, and pear bake together in a creamy, anise-accented sauce.

- **1 cup nonfat milk**
- **1 tablespoon minced fresh ginger**
- **½ teaspoon anise seeds**
- **1¼ pounds parsnips, peeled and thinly sliced**
- **1 small ripe Bosc or Comice pear, peeled, cored, and thinly sliced**
- **1 medium-size onion, thinly sliced**
- **2 cups soft whole wheat bread cubes (you'll need 2 or 3 slices)**
- **Minced parsley**
- **Lemon wedges**

In a 1- to 1½-quart pan, heat milk, ginger, and anise seeds over high heat until steaming; remove from heat.

In a greased shallow 2½- to 3-quart baking dish, layer half each of the parsnips, pear, and onion; then evenly pour half the milk mixture over parsnip mixture. Repeat layers; pour on remaining milk mixture. Cover and bake in a 400° oven for 30 minutes. Meanwhile, whirl bread cubes in a blender or food processor until fine crumbs form.

Uncover baking dish; sprinkle vegetable mixture evenly with crumbs. Continue to bake, uncovered, until crumbs are toasted and parsnips are tender when pierced (about 15 more minutes). Sprinkle with parsley; offer lemon wedges to squeeze over individual servings to taste. Makes 4 to 6 servings.

*Tender baked Parsnips & Pears in Ginger Milk (recipe on facing page),
topped with crisp whole wheat crumbs, and tangy Cranberry-Tomato Relish
in Lemon Shells (recipe on facing page) are perfect complements for a
golden roast chicken. For extra flavor, tuck sage leaves beneath
the bird's skin before roasting.*

71

Stamp Pot with Cabbage

Per serving:
177 calories (6% fat, 81% carbohydrates, 13% protein), 1 g total fat (0.2 g saturated), 37 g carbohydrates, 6 g protein, 0 mg cholesterol, 60 mg sodium

Preparation time: About 35 minutes

Cooking time: About 1 hour

The homey Dutch dishes called *stamppotten* are based on potatoes, but they always include other vegetables as well—in this case, cabbage. In our version, braised-deglazed onions add a rich, sweet flavor to the wholesome combination.

1½ **pounds onions, chopped**
   About 3½ cups low-sodium chicken broth
8 **cups chopped green cabbage (about 2 lbs.)**
2 **pounds russet potatoes**
   Salt and pepper

In a wide frying pan (preferably nonstick), combine onions and ¾ cup of the broth. Cook over high heat, stirring occasionally, until liquid evaporates and onions begin to brown. To deglaze, add ⅓ cup more broth and stir to loosen browned bits; then cook, stirring occasionally, until liquid evaporates and onions begin to brown again. Repeat deglazing step about 4 more times, or until onions are richly browned. Remove from pan; keep warm.

To pan, add cabbage and ½ cup more broth. Cook over high heat, stirring often, until liquid evaporates and cabbage is wilted (about 8 minutes). Return onions to pan; keep mixture warm.

In a 4- to 5-quart pan, bring about 4 cups water to a boil over high heat. Peel potatoes and cut into about 1-inch chunks; add to boiling water. Reduce heat, cover, and boil gently until potatoes are very tender when pierced (about 20 minutes). Drain; then mash with a potato masher (or beat with an electric mixer) until smooth, adding about ⅓ cup broth to give a creamy consistency.

Stir cabbage-onion mixture into potatoes; season to taste with salt and pepper. Makes 6 to 8 servings.

Lean Refried Black Beans

Per serving:
128 calories (24% fat, 52% carbohydrates, 24% protein), 3 g total fat (2 g saturated), 17 g carbohydrates, 8 g protein, 10 mg cholesterol, 369 mg sodium

Preparation time: About 15 minutes

Cooking time: About 30 minutes

Deeply browned onions deglazed with chicken broth contribute to the robust flavor of this cumin-seasoned bean dish. You can prepare the beans up to 2 days ahead of time; to serve, simply heat and top with cheese and cilantro.

1 **large onion, chopped**
2 **cloves garlic, minced or pressed**
1½ **cups low-sodium chicken broth**
2 **cans (about 15 oz. *each*) black beans, drained and rinsed**
½ **teaspoon ground cumin**
⅓ **cup packed feta cheese or queso fresco (available in Hispanic markets)**
   Cilantro sprigs

In a wide frying pan (preferably nonstick), combine onion, garlic, and ¾ cup of the broth. Cook over high heat, stirring occasionally, until liquid evaporates and onion begins to brown. To deglaze, add 2 to 3 tablespoons water and stir to loosen browned bits. Cook, stirring occasionally, until liquid evaporates and onion begins to brown again. Repeat deglazing step, using about 2 tablespoons water each time, until onion is richly browned.

Stir in remaining ¾ cup broth; stir to loosen browned bits. Add beans and cumin. Remove from heat and coarsely mash beans with a large spoon or a potato masher. (At this point, you may cover and refrigerate for up to 2 days.)

Bring bean mixture to a simmer over medium heat. Then simmer, stirring often, for about 15 minutes; beans should be thick enough to hold a fork upright (push beans into a mound to test). Spoon into a serving bowl; crumble cheese over top and garnish with cilantro sprigs. Makes 6 servings.

Barley & Brown Rice Pilaf

Per serving:
236 calories (8% fat, 80% carbohydrates, 12% protein), 2 g total fat (0.5 g saturated), 48 g carbohydrates, 7 g protein, 0 mg cholesterol, 40 mg sodium

Preparation time: About 10 minutes

Cooking time: About 1 hour

Looking for a rice pilaf with a difference? This lean version benefits from the addition of chewy barley; browned onions and a hint of sherry add extra flavor.

- 2 **large onions, chopped**
- 4½ **cups low-sodium chicken broth**
- 1 **cup long-grain brown rice**
- 1 **cup pearl barley, rinsed and drained**
- ½ **teaspoon dry thyme**
- ¼ **cup dry sherry (optional)**
  Salt

In a 3- to 4-quart pan, combine onions and ½ cup of the broth. Cook over high heat, stirring occasionally, until liquid evaporates and onions begin to brown. To deglaze, add 2 to 3 tablespoons water and stir to loosen browned bits. Then cook, stirring occasionally, until liquid evaporates and onions begin to brown again. Repeat deglazing step, using about 2 tablespoons water each time, until onions are richly browned. Scrape onions out of pan.

Rinse and dry pan, then add rice and barley. Cook over medium-high heat, stirring, until grains are dry and smell toasted. Add onions, remaining 4 cups broth, and thyme. Bring to a boil over high heat; then reduce heat to low, cover, and simmer gently until rice and barley are tender to bite (about 40 minutes). Stir in sherry, if desired; season to taste with salt. Makes 6 to 8 servings.

Wild Rice with Aromatics

Per serving:
162 calories (11% fat, 72% carbohydrates, 17% protein), 2 g total fat (0.3 g saturated), 30 g carbohydrates, 7 g protein, 0 mg cholesterol, 34 mg sodium

Preparation time: About 15 minutes

Cooking time: About 1 hour

Welcome company to your home with the fragrance of delicious things to come. A half-dozen spices lend their aromas—and flavors—to wild rice simmered gently in broth.

- 1½ **tablespoons mustard seeds**
- ½ **teaspoon coriander seeds**
- ¼ **teaspoon *each* cumin seeds and whole allspice**
- ⅛ **teaspoon cardamom seeds (pod removed)**
- ½ **teaspoon dry thyme**
- 1 **tablespoon minced fresh ginger**
- 1 **large onion, chopped**
- 4 **cups low-sodium chicken broth**
- 1½ **cups wild rice, rinsed and drained**
  Salt

Pour mustard seeds, coriander seeds, cumin seeds, allspice, and cardamom seeds into a 3- to 4-quart pan. Stir over medium-high heat until seeds are very aromatic (about 1 minute). Add thyme,

ginger, onion, and ¼ cup of the broth. Increase heat to high; cook, stirring, until liquid evaporates and onion begins to brown. To deglaze, add 2 to 3 tablespoons water and stir to loosen browned bits. Then cook, stirring occasionally, until liquid evaporates and onion begins to brown again. Repeat deglazing step, using about 2 tablespoons water each time, until onion is richly browned.

Stir rice and remaining 3¾ cups broth into onion mixture. Bring to a boil over high heat; reduce heat to low, cover, and simmer gently until rice is tender to bite and grains begin to split open (about 45 minutes). Drain; season to taste with salt. Makes 6 to 8 servings.

Teatime is sweet when you serve warm Apple, Cinnamon & Raisin Mini-muffins and baked-ahead Apricot Tea Bread (recipes on page 76). Temptations for snackers of all ages, these quick breads are just as good with fruit juice or icy cold milk as they are with hot tea.

Breads

Crusty, golden brown, and warmly fragrant, homemade bread seems to fulfill some universal longing. Happily, you can satisfy that craving even if you're cutting down on fat. That's because breads, whether from a fine bakery or your own oven, are almost by definition low in fat: many are virtually nothing more than flour, water, and leavening, transformed as if by magic into billowy rolls and loaves. Try your hand at our enticing quick breads, such as tiny bran muffins or fruity Apricot Tea Bread; or bake yeasty Honey Wheat Mini-loaves to delight each guest at your next dinner party. We even tell you how to create savory lowfat pizzas.

Pictured on page 74

Apple, Cinnamon & Raisin Mini-muffins

Per muffin:
72 calories (27% fat, 65% carbohydrates, 8% protein), 2 g total fat (0.3 g saturated), 12 g carbohydrates, 1 g protein, 9 mg cholesterol, 39 mg sodium

Preparation time: About 15 minutes

Baking time: About 20 minutes

Super for snacking, these scaled-down muffins will delight youngsters—and satisfy hungry adults, too. Shredded fresh apple gives the tiny treats their moist texture.

- 1 cup *each* **all-purpose flour and quick-cooking rolled oats**
- 3 tablespoons **firmly packed brown sugar**
- 2 teaspoons **baking powder**
- ½ teaspoon **ground cinnamon**
- 1 **large egg**
- ½ cup **apple juice**
- 3 tablespoons **salad oil**
- 1 **medium-size tart green-skinned apple such as Granny Smith or Newtown Pippin (about 6 oz.), peeled, cored, and shredded**
- ½ cup **raisins**

In a small bowl, mix flour, oats, sugar, baking powder, and cinnamon. In another bowl, combine egg, apple juice, oil, apple, and raisins; beat to mix well. Add dry ingredients and stir just until batter is evenly moistened.

Spoon batter equally into 24 greased tiny (about 1½-inch-diameter) muffin pans. Bake in a 400° oven until well browned (about 20 minutes). Remove from pans; serve warm or cool. If made ahead, let cool completely on racks; then package airtight and hold at room temperature until next day (or freeze for longer storage). Makes 24 muffins.

Pictured on page 74

Apricot Tea Bread

Per serving:
252 calories (20% fat, 73% carbohydrates, 7% protein), 6 g total fat (1 g saturated), 48 g carbohydrates, 5 g protein, 17 mg cholesterol, 115 mg sodium

Preparation time: About 15 minutes

Baking time: About 1 hour

Delicious at teatime (or any time), this quick sour cream–based bread is packed with golden raisins, apricots, and almonds.

- 1 **large egg**
- 2 **large egg whites**
- ¾ cup **sugar**
- ¼ cup **margarine, at room temperature**
- 1 tablespoon **finely shredded orange peel**
- ¼ cup **orange juice**
- ¾ cup **reduced-fat sour cream**
- 2 cups **all-purpose flour**
- 2 teaspoons **baking powder**
- ¼ teaspoon **baking soda**
- 1½ cups **dried apricots (about 10 oz.), cut into pieces**
- 2 cups **golden raisins**
- ¼ cup **sliced almonds**

In a large bowl, combine egg, egg whites, sugar, margarine, and orange peel; beat until blended. Stir in orange juice and sour cream. In a small bowl, mix flour, baking powder, and baking soda; add to egg mixture and beat to blend. Stir in apricots, raisins, and almonds.

Scrape batter into a greased, floured 5- by 9-inch loaf pan (or use a nonstick pan). Spread batter evenly in pan and smooth top.

Bake in a 350° oven until loaf begins to pull away from sides of pan and a wooden skewer inserted in center comes out clean (about 1 hour). Remove from pan; let cool on a rack. If made ahead, let cool completely; then package airtight and hold at room temperature until next day (or freeze for longer storage). Makes 1 loaf (about 16 servings).

Sunflower Soda Bread

Per serving:
148 calories (15% fat, 72% carbohydrates, 13% protein), 2 g total fat (0.4 g saturated), 27 g carbohydrates, 5 g protein, 12 mg cholesterol, 168 mg sodium

Preparation time: About 10 minutes

Baking time: About 25 minutes

This hearty bread, studded with sunflower seeds, is a perfect partner for soup or salad. Our recipe makes two round, golden loaves; you can enjoy one warm from the oven and freeze the second for another meal.

- 2½ **cups all-purpose flour**
- 1 **cup** *each* **whole wheat flour and yellow cornmeal**
- ½ **cup unsalted dry-roasted sunflower seeds**
- ⅓ **cup sugar**
- 2 **teaspoons baking powder**
- 1 **teaspoon baking soda**
- ½ **teaspoon salt**
- 2 **cups buttermilk**
- 1 **large egg, lightly beaten**

In a large bowl, mix all-purpose flour, whole wheat flour, cornmeal, sunflower seeds, sugar, baking powder, baking soda, and salt. Add buttermilk and egg; beat with a heavy spoon until dough is thoroughly moistened and stretchy (about 2 minutes).

Spoon half the dough in a mound in center of a greased 10- by 15-inch baking pan; repeat with remaining dough, using a second baking pan. With floured hands, pat each mound into an 8-inch round. With a floured sharp knife, cut a ½-inch-deep cross on top of each round.

Bake loaves in a 375° oven until golden brown (about 25 minutes; switch positions of pans after 15 minutes). Serve warm or cool, cut into wedges. If made ahead, let cool completely on racks; then package airtight and hold at room temperature until next day (or freeze for longer storage). Makes 2 loaves (8 to 10 servings *each*).

Honey Wheat Mini-loaves

Per serving:
138 calories (12% fat, 77% carbohydrates, 11% protein), 2 g total fat (0.2 g saturated), 27 g carbohydrates, 4 g protein, 0 mg cholesterol, 62 mg sodium

Preparation time: About 25 minutes

Rising time: About 1½ hours

Baking time: About 25 minutes

Little loaves of bread are welcome gifts for just about any occasion. These are perfectly plain and utterly delicious; they're made from a honey-sweetened multigrain yeast dough.

- 1 **package active dry yeast**
- 2 **cups warm water (about 110°F)**
- ¾ **cup honey**
- 3 **tablespoons salad oil**
- 1 **teaspoon salt**
- 2 **cups regular rolled oats**
- 1 **cup multigrain cereal**
- 3 **cups whole wheat flour**
  About 3 cups all-purpose flour

In a large bowl, combine yeast and water; let stand for 5 minutes to soften yeast. Stir in honey, oil, and salt. Beat in oats, cereal, and whole wheat flour. Gradually stir in 3 cups of the all-purpose flour.

Turn dough out onto a floured board and knead until smooth (about 10 minutes), adding more all-purpose flour as needed to prevent sticking. Place dough in an oiled bowl; turn over to grease top. Cover bowl with plastic wrap and let dough rise in a warm place until doubled (about 1 hour).

Punch dough down and divide into sixths. Shape each piece into a loaf; place each in a greased 3- by 5½-inch loaf pan. Cover with plastic wrap and let rise in a warm place until almost doubled (about 30 minutes).

Place pans on a 12- by 15-inch baking sheet. Bake in a 375° oven until loaves are richly browned (about 25 minutes). Remove loaves from pans; let cool on racks. Makes 6 loaves (4 to 6 servings *each*).

Pictured on front cover

Rosemary & Lemon Stretch Breadsticks

Per breadstick:
46 calories (21% fat, 69% carbohydrates, 10% protein), 1 g total fat (0.1 g saturated), 8 g carbohydrates, 1 g protein, 0 mg cholesterol, 69 mg sodium

Preparation time: About 20 minutes

Rising time: About 45 minutes

Baking time: About 20 minutes

Shaping this rosemary-accented bread into sticks is easy, since there's no rolling involved. Just cut the dough into strips, then carefully pull and stretch each one into a long, skinny baton.

> 1 **package active dry yeast**
> 1 **teaspoon sugar**
> 1 **cup warm water (about 110°F)**
> 1 **teaspoon *each* grated lemon peel and salt**
> 1½ **teaspoons chopped fresh rosemary; or 1½ teaspoons dry rosemary, crumbled**
> 2 **tablespoons plus 1 teaspoon olive oil**
> 2½ **to 3 cups all-purpose flour**

In a large bowl, combine yeast, sugar, and water; let stand for 5 minutes to soften yeast. Add lemon peel, salt, rosemary, 2 tablespoons of the oil, and 1½ cups of the flour. Beat with a heavy spoon or an electric mixer until dough is glossy and stretchy (3 to 5 minutes). Then mix in about 1 cup more flour, or enough to make a soft dough.

To knead by hand, scrape dough onto a lightly floured board and knead until smooth and springy (about 10 minutes), adding more flour as needed to prevent sticking.

To knead with a dough hook, beat dough at low to medium speed until it pulls cleanly from sides of bowl and is springy (5 to 7 minutes); if dough is sticky, add more flour, 1 tablespoon at a time.

Turn dough out onto a generously floured board and pat into a 6-inch square. Brush dough with remaining 1 teaspoon oil, loosely cover with plastic wrap, and let rise at room temperature until puffy (about 45 minutes).

Grease 3 large baking sheets. Gently coat dough with 2 tablespoons flour. With a floured sharp knife, cut dough lengthwise into quarters. Work with one quarter at a time. Cut each quarter lengthwise into 8 equal pieces. Pick up one piece and gently stretch it to about 15 inches long; place on a baking sheet. Repeat to shape remaining breadsticks, spacing them at least ½ inch apart on baking sheets.

Bake breadsticks in a 350° oven until golden brown (about 20 minutes), switching positions of baking sheets halfway through baking. If using one oven, refrigerate one sheet of breadsticks, lightly covered, while baking the other two. Lift breadsticks from sheets. Serve; or let cool on racks, then store airtight for up to 3 days. Makes 32 breadsticks.

Tortilla Sticks

Per tortilla stick:
150 calories (2% fat, 86% carbohydrates, 12% protein), 0.4 g total fat (0 g saturated), 31 g carbohydrates, 4 g protein, 0 mg cholesterol, 275 mg sodium

Preparation time: About 25 minutes

Baking time: About 7 minutes

Here's a simple twist on the traditional tortilla—and on the traditional breadstick, too. Just season the breads lightly, roll them into cylinders, and bake until crunchy and golden brown.

> 12 **flour tortillas, *each* about 10 inches in diameter (about 20 oz. *total*)**
> **Salt**

Dip tortillas, one at a time, in water; drain briefly. Season to taste with salt. Then loosely roll each tortilla into a cylinder and fasten with wooden picks.

Place tortilla sticks on 2 greased large baking sheets; bake in a 500° oven until golden on bottom (about 4 minutes). Then turn tortillas over, switch positions of baking sheets, and continue to bake until tortillas are crisp and deep golden (about 3 more minutes). Remove wooden picks. Serve warm or cool. Makes 12 tortilla sticks.

You can reduce the fat in your diet without forgetting your
fondness for pizza! Easy to bake and just the right size for individual
servings, our colorful Yellow Bell Pizza and hearty Spinach Pizza (recipes
on page 80) make a delightful supper. Serve them with a leafy salad
and a bottle of robust red wine.

Lowfat Pizzas

Cutting down on fat doesn't mean cutting out pizza. The four recipes here are sure to satisfy with their savory toppings and hearty, chewy crusts.

If you like, you can save time by starting with frozen bread dough; we suggest covering it with fresh bell peppers (and just a bit of mozzarella cheese) or with shallots, spinach, and a little Jarlsberg. Or try a homemade whole wheat crust, crowned with your choice of two toppings: artichoke hearts and sweet onions braised in broth, or a colorful mixture of zucchini, crookneck squash, and cherry tomatoes.

Pictured on page 79

Yellow Bell Pizza

Preparation time: About 20 minutes
Rising time: About 20 minutes
Baking time: About 16 minutes

- 1 loaf (about 1 lb.) frozen white bread dough, thawed
- 1 cup (about 4 oz.) shredded part-skim mozzarella cheese
- 2 medium-size yellow bell peppers (about 12 oz. *total*), seeded and thinly sliced
- 4 teaspoons grated Parmesan cheese
- 1 tablespoon chopped fresh basil or 1 teaspoon dry basil

Cut dough into quarters. Shape each piece into a ball; on a lightly floured board, roll out each ball to make a 6-inch-diameter round. Place rounds, about 1 inch apart, on 2 lightly oiled 12- by 15-inch baking sheets. With your hands, flatten rounds to about ¼ inch thick (make edges slightly thicker) and 7 inches wide. Let stand, uncovered, at room temperature until puffy (about 20 minutes).

Sprinkle each round to within ¼ inch of edges with 2 tablespoons of the mozzarella cheese; top rounds equally with bell peppers. Then sprinkle evenly with remaining ½ cup mozzarella cheese, Parmesan cheese, and basil.

Bake pizzas in a 400° oven until crust is brown on bottom; lift to check (about 16 minutes; switch positions of baking sheets after 8 minutes). To serve, cut hot pizzas into quarters. Makes 4 servings.

Per serving: 355 calories (19% fat, 62% carbohydrates, 19% protein), 7 g total fat (3 g saturated), 56 g carbohydrates, 17 g protein, 18 mg cholesterol, 823 mg sodium

Pictured on page 79

Spinach Pizza

Preparation time: About 20 minutes
Rising time: About 20 minutes
Baking time: About 16 minutes

- 1 loaf (about 1 lb.) frozen white bread dough, thawed
- ¼ cup chopped shallots
- ½ cup low-sodium chicken broth
- 2 packages (about 10 oz. *each*) frozen chopped spinach, thawed and squeezed dry
- ¼ teaspoon ground nutmeg
- ½ cup shredded reduced-fat Jarlsberg cheese

Cut dough into quarters. Shape each piece into a ball; on a lightly floured board, roll out each ball to make a 6-inch-diameter round. Place rounds, about 1 inch apart, on 2 lightly oiled 12- by 15-inch baking sheets. With your hands, flatten rounds to about ¼ inch thick (make edges slightly thicker) and 7 inches wide. Let stand, uncovered, at room temperature until puffy (about 20 minutes).

While dough is rising, combine shallots and broth in a wide frying pan. Cook over medium-high heat, stirring occasionally, until shallots are soft and golden and all liquid has evaporated (about 10 minutes). Add spinach and nutmeg to shallots and mix until well blended. Remove from heat and let cool.

Cover each round to within ¼ inch of edges with a fourth of the spinach mixture; then sprinkle rounds evenly with cheese.

Bake pizzas in a 400° oven until crust is brown on bottom; lift to check (about 16 minutes; switch positions of baking sheets after 8 minutes). To serve, cut hot pizzas into quarters. Makes 4 servings.

Per serving: 346 calories (13% fat, 67% carbohydrates, 20% protein), 5 g total fat (1 g saturated), 58 g carbohydrates, 17 g protein, 6 mg cholesterol, 832 mg sodium

Sweet Onion Pizza

Preparation time: About 45 minutes
Rising time: About 1 hour
Baking time: About 25 minutes

- 1 package active dry yeast
- 1¼ cups warm water (about 110°F)
- 1½ tablespoons olive oil
- 1 teaspoon *each* sugar and salt
- 1½ cups whole wheat flour
  About 1½ cups all-purpose flour
- 3 large onions, thinly sliced
- ½ cup low-sodium chicken broth
- 4 medium-size pear-shaped (Roma-type) tomatoes, thinly sliced
- 1 package (about 10 oz.) frozen artichoke hearts, thawed
- 1 cup (about 4 oz.) crumbled feta cheese
- 1 tablespoon fresh oregano leaves or 1 teaspoon dry oregano

In a large bowl, combine yeast and water; let stand for 5 minutes to soften yeast. Add oil, sugar, salt, and whole wheat flour. Beat with a heavy spoon or an electric mixer until flour is moistened.

To knead by hand, stir in 1½ cups of the all-purpose flour with a heavy spoon. Scrape dough onto a lightly floured board and knead until smooth and elastic (about 5 minutes), adding more all-purpose flour as needed to prevent sticking.

To knead with a dough hook, mix in 1 cup of the all-purpose flour. Beat at medium speed until dough is smooth and elastic (about 3 minutes); if dough is sticky, add more all-purpose flour, 1 tablespoon at a time.

Place dough in an oiled bowl and turn over to grease top. Cover with plastic wrap; let dough rise in a warm place until doubled (about 1 hour).

While dough is rising, combine onions and broth in a wide frying pan. Cook over medium-high heat, stirring occasionally, until onions are soft and golden and all liquid has evaporated (about 30 minutes). Remove from heat and let cool.

Punch dough down, turn out onto a floured board, and roll out to a 15-inch-diameter round. Transfer to a lightly greased 14-inch pizza pan; roll edges in to form a rim. Cover dough with onions; then top with tomatoes and artichokes. Sprinkle with cheese and oregano.

Bake pizza in a 425° oven until edges of crust are golden (about 25 minutes). To serve, cut into wedges in pan. Makes 8 servings.

Per serving: 277 calories (21% fat, 65% carbohydrates, 14% protein), 7 g total fat (3 g saturated), 47 g carbohydrates, 10 g protein, 13 mg cholesterol, 463 mg sodium

Summer Squash Pizza

Preparation time: About 45 minutes
Rising time: About 1 hour
Baking time: About 25 minutes

- 1 package active dry yeast
- 1¼ cups warm water (about 110°F)
- 1½ tablespoons olive oil
- 1 teaspoon *each* sugar and salt
- 1½ cups whole wheat flour
  About 1½ cups all-purpose flour
- 1 pound *each* zucchini and crookneck squash, thinly sliced
- 1 clove garlic, minced or pressed
- 1 tablespoon fresh oregano leaves or 1 teaspoon dry oregano
- ½ cup low-sodium chicken broth
- 1 pound cherry tomatoes (about 3 cups), cut into halves
- ¼ cup grated Parmesan cheese

In a large bowl, combine yeast and water; let stand for 5 minutes to soften yeast. Add oil, sugar, salt, and whole wheat flour. Beat with a heavy spoon or an electric mixer until flour is moistened.

To knead by hand, stir in 1½ cups of the all-purpose flour with a heavy spoon. Scrape dough onto a lightly floured board and knead until smooth and elastic (about 5 minutes), adding more all-purpose flour as needed to prevent sticking.

To knead with a dough hook, mix in 1 cup of the all-purpose flour. Beat at medium speed until dough is smooth and elastic (about 3 minutes); if dough is sticky, add more all-purpose flour, 1 tablespoon at a time.

Place dough in an oiled bowl and turn over to grease top. Cover with plastic wrap; let dough rise in a warm place until doubled (about 1 hour).

While dough is rising, combine zucchini, crookneck squash, garlic, oregano, and broth in a wide frying pan. Cook over medium-high heat, stirring occasionally, until all liquid has evaporated (about 20 minutes). Remove from heat and let cool.

Punch dough down, turn out onto a floured board, and roll out to a 15-inch-diameter round. Transfer to a lightly greased 14-inch pizza pan; roll edges in to form a rim. Cover dough with squash mixture; then top with tomatoes, cut side up. Sprinkle with cheese.

Bake pizza in a 425° oven until edges of crust are golden (about 25 minutes). To serve, cut into wedges in pan. Makes 8 servings.

Per serving: 234 calories (16% fat, 69% carbohydrates, 15% protein), 4 g total fat (1 g saturated), 42 g carbohydrates, 9 g protein, 2 mg cholesterol, 334 mg sodium

Pour strawberry purée over servings of Honeydew Melon Dessert Bowl (recipe on page 84) for a refreshing buffet-style dessert. Chewy, chocolate-dotted Graham Cracker Crackle Cookies (recipe on page 92) are a sweet complement to the fruit.

Desserts

Luscious sweets and lowfat desserts can be one and the same thing when you choose the recipes we offer here. Do you crave a homey fruit treat, warm from the oven? Then consider Amaretti, Nectarine & Blueberry Crumble or Baked Pears with Ginger. Or would you rather scoop up spoonfuls of Mango Sorbet from Cookie Tulips? Perhaps you'd like to tantalize the family with Berry Yogurt Cheese Pie, nestled in a crisp graham crust and topped with juicy ripe raspberries. Whatever your selection, you're bound to be delighted. As a bonus, this chapter also includes two pages of superb lowfat breakfast specialties.

Pictured on page 82

Honeydew Melon Dessert Bowl

Per serving:
116 **calories** *(3% fat, 94% carbohydrates, 3% protein), 0.5 g* **total fat** *(0 g saturated), 30 g* **carbohydrates**, *1 g* **protein**, *0 mg* **cholesterol**, *37 mg* **sodium***

Preparation time: About 30 minutes

Hollow out two honeydew melons to use as serving bowls for this easy three-color fruit salad. To dress up each portion, top it with a lightly sweetened fresh strawberry purée. (You'll find canned litchis in Asian markets and some well-stocked supermarkets.)

   2   **medium-size honeydew melons (2½ to 3½ lbs.** *each***)**
   1   **large can (about 20 oz.) or 2 cans (about 11 oz.** *each***) litchis**
  10   **to 16 strawberries, hulled and halved**
       Strawberry Sauce (recipe follows)
       Mint sprigs

Set each melon on the side where it rests most steadily; then cut off top third of each melon. Scoop out and discard seeds; scoop fruit in balls or chunks from shells and from top slices, removing as much melon as possible. Discard top slices.

Place melon pieces in a bowl. Drain litchis, reserving ½ cup of the syrup for Strawberry Sauce (discard remaining syrup). Add litchis and straw-

berries to melon pieces; mix gently. Spoon fruit into melon shells. Prepare Strawberry Sauce. (At this point, you may cover and refrigerate fruit salad and sauce separately for up to 4 hours.)

Garnish fruit in melon shells with mint sprigs. To serve, ladle fruit into bowls and top with Strawberry Sauce. Makes 8 to 10 servings.

Strawberry Sauce. In a blender or food processor, combine 3 cups **strawberries** (hulled), the ½ cup **reserved litchi syrup,** 2 tablespoons **lemon juice,** and about 1 tablespoon **sugar** (or to taste). Whirl until smooth.

Baked Pears with Ginger

Per serving:
167 **calories** *(3% fat, 95% carbohydrates, 2% protein), 0.7 g* **total fat** *(0 g saturated), 43 g* **carbohydrates**, *0.7 g* **protein**, *0 mg* **cholesterol**, *9 mg* **sodium***

Preparation time: About 10 minutes

Baking time: 1 to 1¼ hours

Baked with a little sugar and a generous helping of crystallized ginger, these juicy whole pears are delightful for a cool-weather dessert. You might serve the spicy fruit with spoonfuls of vanilla frozen yogurt.

   6   **medium-size firm-ripe Bosc or Bartlett pears (about 2½ lbs.** *total***)**
   ¾   **cup water**
   1   **tablespoon lemon juice**
   2   **tablespoons sugar**
   ⅓   **cup minced crystallized ginger**
       Vanilla lowfat frozen yogurt (optional)

If necessary, trim bottoms of pears so they will stand upright. Fit pears snugly into a shallow 1½- to 2-quart baking dish or pan (such as an 8-inch-square baking pan). In a small bowl, mix water and lemon juice; pour over pears. Sprinkle with sugar.

Bake, uncovered, in a 450° oven for 30 minutes; then reduce oven temperature to 400°. Baste pears with pan juices, sprinkle with ginger, and continue to bake, basting occasionally, until pears are richly browned and tender when pierced (30 to 45 more minutes). Serve warm or cool; top with frozen yogurt, if desired. Makes 6 servings.

Dessert Nachos with Fruit Salsa

Per serving:
240 **calories** *(20% fat, 71% carbohydrates, 9% protein), 5 g* **total fat** *(3 g saturated), 44 g* **carbohydrates**, *6 g* **protein**, *16 mg* **cholesterol**, *276 mg* **sodium**

Preparation time: About 25 minutes

Baking time: About 8 minutes

Nachos and salsa for dessert? Absolutely—when the crisp tortilla wedges are dusted with cinnamon sugar and the salsa is a sweet blend of diced fruits. Offer a honey-orange cream cheese sauce alongside, too.

>   **Fruit Salsa (recipe follows)**
> ⅓ **cup sugar**
> 1   **teaspoon ground cinnamon**
> 10 **flour tortillas (*each* 7 to 8 inches in diameter)**
> 1   **large package (about 8 oz.) Neufchâtel cheese**
> ½   **cup orange juice**
> 3   **tablespoons honey**

Prepare Fruit Salsa; cover and refrigerate until ready to serve (or for up to 4 hours).

In a shallow bowl, mix sugar and cinnamon. Working with one tortilla at a time, brush both sides lightly with water; then cut tortilla into 6 equal wedges. Dip one side of each wedge in sugar mixture. Arrange wedges in a single layer, sugared sides up, on oiled foil-lined baking sheets. Bake, one sheet at a time, in a 500° oven until tortilla wedges are crisp and golden (about 4 minutes). Remove wedges from baking sheets and let cool slightly on racks.

While tortillas are baking, in a 1- to 2-quart pan, combine Neufchâtel cheese, orange juice, and honey. Whisk over low heat until sauce is smooth (about 3 minutes).

To serve, mound warm tortilla wedges on a platter. Offer sauce and Fruit Salsa to spoon onto wedges. Makes 10 to 12 servings.

Fruit Salsa. Hull 2 cups **strawberries;** dice into a bowl. Add 2 large **kiwi fruit** (about 8 oz. *total*), peeled and diced, and 1 can (about 11 oz.) **mandarin oranges,** drained.

Amaretti, Nectarine & Blueberry Crumble

Per serving:
264 **calories** *(15% fat, 80% carbohydrates, 5% protein), 4 g* **total fat** *(0.6 g saturated), 56 g* **carbohydrates**, *4 g* **protein**, *0 mg* **cholesterol**, *53 mg* **sodium**

Preparation time: About 25 minutes

Baking time: About 55 minutes

Luscious summer fruits make a delightfully simple dessert to present warm from the oven. If you like, top each serving with a scoop of frozen yogurt.

> 8   **large nectarines (about 2½ lbs. *total*)**
> 2   **cups fresh or frozen blueberries**
> ⅓ **cup granulated sugar**
> ¼   **teaspoon ground nutmeg**
> 2   **tablespoons lemon juice**
> ⅓ **cup firmly packed brown sugar**
> 2   **tablespoons margarine, diced**
> 1   **large egg white**
> ⅔ **cup coarsely crushed almond macaroons (about 10 cookies, *each* 1¾ inches in diameter)**
> ½   **cup quick-cooking rolled oats**
>   **Vanilla lowfat frozen yogurt (optional)**

Pit nectarines; then cut into ½-inch-thick slices (you should have about 8 cups). In a shallow 2½- to 3-quart casserole, combine nectarines, blueberries, granulated sugar, and nutmeg; mix lightly, then drizzle with lemon juice.

In a medium-size bowl, combine brown sugar, margarine, and egg white; stir until well combined. Mix in macaroon crumbs and oats. Spoon crumb mixture evenly over fruit in casserole.

Bake in a 375° oven until crumb topping is well browned, fruit mixture is bubbly, and nectarines in center of casserole are tender when pierced (about 55 minutes). Let cool for at least 10 minutes; serve warm. Top with frozen yogurt, if desired. Makes 6 to 8 servings.

Ruby Grapefruit Terrine with Tea Sauce

Per serving:
96 *calories* (2% fat, 89% carbohydrates, 9% protein), 0.2 g *total fat* (0 g saturated), 23 g *carbohydrates*, 2 g *protein*, 0 mg *cholesterol*, 4 mg *sodium*

Preparation time: *About 1 hour*

Chilling time: *At least 8 hours*

Terrines are typically savory dishes of meat or vegetables, but this one's a marvelously refreshing grapefruit dessert. Serve each slice in a pool of citrusy tea sauce.

- **8 or 9 large red grapefruit (about 1 lb. *each*)**
- **3 tablespoons frozen orange juice concentrate, thawed**
- **1 tablespoon sugar**
- **1 tablespoon unflavored gelatin (about 1½ envelopes)**
- **Tea Sauce (recipe follows)**

Cut peel and all white membrane from 8 of the grapefruit. Holding fruit over a bowl to catch juice, cut segments free and drop into bowl. Carefully drain juice from bowl; then measure juice and segments. You need 2½ cups juice and 6 cups segments; if necessary, segment or squeeze another grapefruit.

Set aside 8 to 10 of the best-looking segments to use for garnish; cover and refrigerate until ready to use. In a 4½- by 8-inch metal loaf pan, neatly layer remaining segments to within ½ inch of pan rim.

In a 1- to 2-quart pan, blend 1 cup of the grapefruit juice (reserve remainder for sauce), orange juice concentrate, sugar, and gelatin. Let stand for 5 minutes to soften gelatin; stir over low heat until gelatin is dissolved. Pour gelatin mixture over grapefruit in pan. Cover; refrigerate until firm (at least 8 hours) or for up to 1 day. Prepare Tea Sauce.

To serve, dip chilled terrine briefly in hot water to within ½ inch of pan rim. Uncover terrine. Invert a platter over pan; holding pan and platter together, invert both. Lift off pan. Pour equal portions of Tea Sauce on 8 to 10 dessert plates. With a sharp knife, carefully cut terrine into 8 to 10 equal slices. Set slices on sauce; garnish with reserved grapefruit segments. Makes 8 to 10 servings.

Tea Sauce. In a 2- to 3-quart pan, mix 1½ cups **grapefruit juice** and 2 tablespoons **sugar.** Bring to a boil over medium-high heat. Add 1 tablespoon **black tea leaves;** reduce heat, cover, and simmer for 5 minutes. Pour mixture through a fine strainer.

Mix 1 tablespoon **cornstarch** with 2 tablespoons **cold water;** stir into tea mixture. Bring to a boil over medium-high heat, stirring; let cool.

Pictured on facing page

Bing Cherry Flan

Per serving:
174 *calories* (8% fat, 74% carbohydrates, 18% protein), 2 g *total fat* (0.4 g saturated), 33 g *carbohydrates*, 8 g *protein*, 38 mg *cholesterol*, 102 mg *sodium*

Preparation time: *About 15 minutes*

Baking time: *About 45 minutes*

In central France, this custardy fruit dessert is known as *clafoutis*. It can be made with a variety of fresh fruits, but plump, glossy dark sweet cherries are the traditional first choice.

- **Vegetable oil cooking spray**
- **2 cups dark sweet cherries, stemmed and pitted**
- **2 tablespoons kirsch or brandy**
- **2 tablespoons all-purpose flour**
- **⅓ cup granulated sugar**
- **⅛ teaspoon ground nutmeg**
- **1 large egg**
- **2 large egg whites**
- **1½ cups evaporated skim milk**
- **1 teaspoon vanilla**
- **2 tablespoons powdered sugar**

Spray a 10-inch quiche dish or other shallow 1½-quart baking dish with cooking spray. Spread cherries in dish; drizzle with kirsch and set aside.

In a medium-size bowl, mix flour, granulated sugar, and nutmeg. Beat in egg, then egg whites; gradually stir in milk and vanilla. Pour egg mixture over cherries. Bake in a 350° oven until custard is puffed and golden brown, and a knife inserted in center comes out clean (about 45 minutes). Let cool slightly, then sift powdered sugar over top. Cut into wedges and serve warm. Makes 6 servings.

*For an easy summertime fresh fruit treat, bake simple Bing Cherry Flan
(recipe on facing page). This country-style pudding tastes best warm from the
oven; sprinkle it with powdered sugar just before serving.*

Lowfat Breakfasts

If you choose the right recipes—or revise your old faithfuls—you'll find that many breakfast favorites fit nicely into a lowfat regime. On these pages, we offer six delicious examples.

Apple Oatmeal Waffles

Preparation time: About 15 minutes
Cooking time: About 20 minutes

 1 cup regular rolled oats
1⅔ cups all-purpose flour
2½ teaspoons baking powder
 1 teaspoon ground cinnamon
 ½ teaspoon salt (optional)
 1 cup nonfat milk
 ¼ cup maple syrup
 ¼ cup orange juice or apple juice
 1 large egg, lightly beaten
 3 large egg whites
 ¾ cup peeled, chopped tart apple
 ½ cup raisins

Spread oats in an 8- or 9-inch baking pan and bake in a 350° oven until golden (about 12 minutes), stirring occasionally. Remove from oven, pour into a large bowl, and stir in flour, baking powder, cinnamon, and salt (if used).

In another bowl, beat milk, syrup, orange juice, egg, and egg whites. Stir in apple and raisins; add to flour mixture and stir until moistened.

Preheat a waffle iron according to manufacturer's directions. Grease iron, then fill three-fourths full of batter. Bake until waffles are golden and crisp (about 6 minutes). Keep warm on a rack in a 200° oven. Repeat to bake remaining batter. Makes 12 waffles (*each* about 4 inches square).

Per waffle: 149 calories (6% fat, 80% carbohydrates, 14% protein), 1 g total fat (0.2 g saturated), 30 g carbohydrates, 5 g protein, 18 mg cholesterol, 120 mg sodium

Cornmeal Crêpes with Berries

Preparation time: About 20 minutes
Cooking time: About 15 minutes

 3 cups hulled, sliced strawberries
 2 tablespoons sugar
 1 cup nonfat milk
 3 large eggs
 ⅔ cup all-purpose flour
 ¼ cup yellow cornmeal
 1 teaspoon vanilla
   About 2½ teaspoons margarine
   About ¼ cup apricot jam
   Vanilla nonfat or lowfat yogurt

In a small bowl, gently mix strawberries and sugar; set aside.

In a blender, combine milk, eggs, flour, cornmeal, and vanilla; whirl until smooth.

Place a flat-bottomed 7- to 8-inch frying pan or crêpe pan over medium-high heat. When pan is hot, add ¼ teaspoon of the margarine and swirl to coat surface. Pour in ¼ cup of the batter all at once; quickly tilt pan so batter flows over entire surface (don't worry if there are a few holes). Cook until surface of crêpe is dry and edges are lightly browned (about 1 minute). Turn crêpe over with a spatula and brown other side; then turn out onto a plate and keep warm. Repeat to cook remaining batter, stirring batter thoroughly before cooking each crêpe (cornmeal tends to sink to bottom of bowl). Stack crêpes as made.

Spread one side of each crêpe lightly with jam; fold crêpe in quarters. Serve crêpes with berries and yogurt. Makes 4 servings (8 to 10 crêpes).

Per serving: 323 calories (19% fat, 68% carbohydrates, 13% protein), 7 g total fat (2 g saturated), 55 g carbohydrates, 10 g protein, 161 mg cholesterol, 111 mg sodium

Breakfast Rice, Oats & Granola

Preparation time: About 5 minutes
Cooking time: About 40 minutes

 1 cup long-grain brown rice
4¾ cups water
 1 cup regular rolled oats
1¼ teaspoons ground cinnamon
 1 teaspoon vanilla
 ½ teaspoon ground nutmeg
1¾ cups granola cereal
   Condiments: Nonfat milk, raisins, chopped dates or other dried fruit, chopped nuts, honey, maple syrup, and/or brown sugar

In a 1½- to 2-quart pan, combine rice and 2½ cups of the water. Bring to a boil over high heat; then reduce heat to medium and boil gently, uncovered, until almost all water has evaporated (about 15 minutes). Reduce heat to low, cover, and continue to cook until rice is tender to bite (about 15 more minutes). Spoon rice from pan into a large bowl; set aside.

In same pan, bring remaining 2¼ cups water to a boil. Add oats, cinnamon, vanilla, and nutmeg. Reduce heat to low and cook, stirring, until oats are tender to bite (about 5 minutes). Mix cooked oatmeal and granola with rice.

Serve cereal hot, with condiments to add to taste. Makes 6 servings (about 1 cup *each*).

Per serving: 329 calories (23% fat, 67% carbohydrates, 10% protein), 8 g total fat (4 g saturated), 55 g carbohydrates, 8 g protein, 0 mg cholesterol, 17 mg sodium

Breakfast Focaccia

Preparation time: About 20 minutes
Rising time: About 45 minutes
Baking time: About 40 minutes

1 loaf (about 1 lb.) frozen white bread dough, thawed
1½ tablespoons margarine, melted
3 large firm-ripe plums (about 1 lb. *total*), pitted and cut into ¼-inch-thick slices; or 3 cups thinly sliced apples
3 tablespoons sugar
1 teaspoon ground cinnamon

Place bread dough in a lightly oiled 10- by 15-inch baking pan. Stretch and press to fill pan evenly. (If dough is too elastic to stay in place, let rest for a few minutes, then press out.) Cover dough lightly with plastic wrap and let rise in a warm place until puffy (about 45 minutes).

Brush dough with 1 tablespoon of the margarine. Arrange plum slices, without overlapping, on dough. Brush fruit with remaining 1½ teaspoons margarine; mix sugar and cinnamon and sprinkle over fruit.

Bake focaccia on bottom rack of a 350° oven until well browned on edges and bottom; lift gently with a spatula to check (about 40 minutes). Serve warm. If made ahead, let cool; then wrap airtight and hold at room temperature until next day. Reheat, uncovered, in a 350° oven until warm to the touch (5 to 10 minutes). Makes 6 servings.

Per serving: 260 calories (16% fat, 74% carbohydrates, 10% protein), 5 g total fat (0.5 g saturated), 49 g carbohydrates, 6 g protein, 0 mg cholesterol, 473 mg sodium

Apricot-Ricotta Spread

Preparation time: About 15 minutes

¼ cup chopped dried apricots
3 tablespoons orange juice
1 cup part-skim ricotta cheese
3 tablespoons honey
½ teaspoon ground coriander
   Whole wheat bagels, split and toasted

In a small bowl, soak apricots in orange juice until soft (about 10 minutes). In a food processor or blender, combine apricot mixture, ricotta cheese, honey, and coriander; whirl until well blended. If made ahead, cover and refrigerate for up to 3 days.

Serve cheese spread cold or at room temperature, with toasted bagels. Makes about 1¼ cups (4 to 6 servings).

Per serving: 126 calories (27% fat, 55% carbohydrates, 18% protein), 4 g total fat (2 g saturated), 18 g carbohydrates, 6 g protein, 15 mg cholesterol, 63 mg sodium

Cinnamon Apples with Frozen Yogurt

Preparation time: About 30 minutes
Baking time: About 30 minutes

¼ cup margarine, cut up
2 tablespoons water
½ cup firmly packed brown sugar
1 tablespoon lemon juice
1 teaspoon ground cinnamon
4 large Golden Delicious apples (about 2 lbs. *total*), peeled, cored, and thinly sliced
1 to 2 pints vanilla lowfat frozen yogurt

Place margarine in a 10- by 15-inch baking pan and set in a 400° oven until melted (about 1½ minutes). Stir in water, sugar, lemon juice, and cinnamon; then add apples and stir to coat with sugar mixture. Bake, uncovered, until apples are slightly tender when pierced (about 25 minutes). Serve apple mixture warm, with scoops of frozen yogurt. Makes 4 to 6 servings.

Per serving: 373 calories (25% fat, 69% carbohydrates, 6% protein), 11 g total fat (2 g saturated), 66 g carbohydrates, 5 g protein, 6 mg cholesterol, 180 mg sodium

Garnished with jewel-bright fruits and sprigs of mint, Mango Sorbet in Cookie Tulips (recipe on facing page) concludes a company meal with a delicious flourish. Because the tropical fruit ice and crisp cookie bowls can both be made ahead, presenting the dessert is a breeze.

Pictured on facing page

Mango Sorbet in Cookie Tulips

Per serving:
378 **calories** (19% fat, 78% carbohydrates, 3% protein), 8 g **total fat** (1 g saturated), 76 g **carbohydrates**, 3 g **protein**, 0 mg **cholesterol**, 168 mg **sodium**

Preparation time: About 1 hour

Baking time: About 30 minutes

A special meal deserves a dramatic finale: scoops of vivid mango sorbet served in crisp cookie shells and garnished with your choice of fresh fruit. (When you plan your cooking schedule, be sure to allow ample time for freezing the sorbet.)

- 4 **medium-size ripe mangoes (about 2¾ lbs. *total*)**
- ⅔ **cup light corn syrup**
- ½ **cup lemon juice**
  Cookie Tulips (recipe follows)
  Fresh fruit and mint sprigs (optional)

Peel mangoes; slice fruit from pits and place in a blender or food processor. Add corn syrup and lemon juice; whirl until smooth. Pour mixture into an ice cream maker and freeze according to manufacturer's directions. If made ahead, scoop into a container, cover, and freeze for up to 1 week.

While sorbet is freezing, prepare Cookie Tulips.

To serve, scoop sorbet into Cookie Tulips; garnish with fruit and mint, if desired. Makes 6 servings.

Cookie Tulips. In a medium-size bowl, beat ¼ cup **margarine,** at room temperature, and ½ cup **sugar** until smooth. Add 7 tablespoons **all-purpose flour,** 1 teaspoon **vanilla,** and 2 large **egg whites;** mix until smooth.

Bake cookies 2 at a time. Grease a 12- by 15-inch baking sheet. With fingertip, draw a 7-inch circle in one corner of sheet; repeat in opposite corner. Place 3 tablespoons of the batter in each circle and spread to fill evenly. Bake cookies in a 350° oven until golden (about 9 minutes). At once, using a wide spatula, lift cookies, one at a time, from sheet; drape each over a clean 1-pound food can and gently pinch sides to form a fluted cup. Let cookies cool until firm; then carefully lift from cans.

Repeat to bake 4 more cookies. If made ahead, let cool completely; store airtight for up to 1 day. Makes 6 cookies.

Blueberry Buttermilk Sherbet

Per serving:
77 **calories** (6% fat, 86% carbohydrates, 8% protein), 0.5 g **total fat** (0.2 g saturated), 17 g **carbohydrates**, 2 g **protein**, 2 mg **cholesterol**, 47 mg **sodium**

Preparation time: About 20 minutes

Chilling & freezing time: At least 5½ hours

Only five ingredients go into this tangy sherbet, just right for dessert on a sultry summer evening. You can use either fresh or frozen berries.

- 2 **cups fresh or frozen blueberries**
- 2 **teaspoons grated lemon peel**
- 2 **tablespoons lemon juice**
- ¼ **cup sugar**
- 1 **cup lowfat buttermilk**

In a 2- to 3-quart pan, combine blueberries, lemon peel, lemon juice, and sugar. Cook over medium-high heat, stirring often, until mixture comes to a simmer and berries begin to pop (about 6 minutes).

Cover and refrigerate until cool (at least 1 hour) or until next day.

In a blender or food processor, combine blueberry mixture and buttermilk; whirl until smoothly puréed. Pour into a 9- or 10-inch-square metal pan, cover, and freeze until solid (at least 4 hours).

Break blueberry mixture into chunks; whirl in a food processor (or beat with an electric mixer) until smooth. Return to pan, cover, and freeze until firm (at least 30 minutes) or for up to 1 week. Let hard-frozen sherbet soften slightly before serving. Makes about 6 servings (about ½ cup *each*).

Whole Wheat Orange Bars

Per bar:
211 **calories** *(21% fat, 71% carbohydrates, 8% protein), 5 g* **total fat** *(0.9 g saturated), 39 g* **carbohydrates,** *4 g* **protein,** *35 mg* **cholesterol,** *143 mg* **sodium**

Preparation time: About 25 minutes

Baking time: About 35 minutes

These hearty bars are studded with chopped dates and juicy chunks of fresh orange. Before cooling and cutting the cookies, spread them with a simple orange frosting.

- 1 **large orange (8 to 10 oz.)**
- 1 **cup** *each* **whole wheat flour and all-purpose flour**
- ½ **cup chopped pitted dates**
- 2 **tablespoons sugar**
- 1 **teaspoon baking soda**
- ½ **teaspoon baking powder**
- 1 **can (about 6 oz.) frozen orange juice concentrate, thawed**
- ¼ **cup margarine, melted**
- 2 **large eggs, lightly beaten**
  Orange Frosting (recipe follows)

Cut peel and all white membrane from orange; then cut fruit into ½-inch chunks and remove seeds. Set aside.

In a medium-size bowl, stir together whole wheat flour, all-purpose flour, dates, sugar, baking soda, and baking powder. Reserve 1 tablespoon of the orange juice concentrate for frosting; pour remaining concentrate into a large bowl and mix in margarine and eggs.

Add flour mixture and orange pieces to egg mixture; stir just until batter is evenly moistened. Spread batter in a greased 9-inch-square baking pan and bake in a 350° oven just until cookies pull from pan sides (about 35 minutes).

Prepare Orange Frosting and spread over hot cookies; let cool. To serve, cut into 12 rectangles. Makes 12 bars.

Orange Frosting. In a small bowl, combine ¾ cup **powdered sugar,** the 1 tablespoon **reserved orange juice concentrate,** and 1 tablespoon **water.** Beat until smooth.

Pictured on page 82

Graham Cracker Crackle Cookies

Per cookie:
64 **calories** *(14% fat, 82% carbohydrates, 4% protein), 1 g* **total fat** *(0.4 g saturated), 13 g* **carbohydrates,** *0.7 g* **protein,** *0.3 mg* **cholesterol,** *35 mg* **sodium**

Preparation time: About 20 minutes

Baking time: About 7 minutes

Dotted with semisweet chocolate chips, these crunchy cookies are made with graham cracker crumbs—and malted milk powder for flavor.

- 1 **large egg white**
- ⅛ **teaspoon cream of tartar**
- 1¼ **cups powdered sugar**
- 2 **tablespoons malted milk powder**
- ½ **cup graham cracker crumbs**
- ¼ **cup semisweet chocolate chips**

In a large bowl, mix egg white, cream of tartar, sugar, and malted milk powder. Beat with an electric mixer at high speed until thick and smooth. Stir in graham cracker crumbs.

Drop dough in 1½-teaspoon mounds 3 inches apart on 3 oiled, floured 12- by 15-inch nonstick baking sheets (or use regular baking sheets, lightly coated with vegetable oil cooking spray, then floured). Lightly press chocolate chips equally into mounds.

Bake cookies in a 375° oven until golden brown (about 7 minutes; switch positions of baking sheets after 4 minutes). Let cookies cool on baking sheets for 1 minute; then transfer with a spatula to racks. If made ahead, let cool; then store airtight for up to 3 days. Makes about 18 cookies.

Berry Yogurt Cheese Pie

Per serving:
341 *calories* (24% fat, 57% carbohydrates, 19% protein), 9 g *total fat* (1 g saturated), 48 g *carbohydrates*, 16 g *protein*, 7 mg *cholesterol*, 496 mg *sodium*

Preparation time: About 40 minutes

Chilling time: At least 16 hours

Tangy homemade yogurt cheese and plenty of cottage cheese go into the smooth, lime-accented filling for this berry-topped pie.

- 4 **cups plain nonfat yogurt**
  Graham Crust (recipe follows)
- 1 **envelope unflavored gelatin**
- ¼ **cup water**
- 2 **cups nonfat or lowfat cottage cheese**
- ½ **cup sugar**
- 1½ **teaspoons grated lime peel**
- 2 **tablespoons lime juice**
- 2 **cups raspberries or hulled, sliced strawberries**

Line a fine strainer with muslin or a double layer of cheesecloth. Set strainer over a deep bowl (bottom of strainer should sit at least 2 inches above bottom of bowl). Spoon yogurt into cloth. Cover airtight and refrigerate until yogurt is firm (at least 12 hours) or for up to 2 days; occasionally pour off liquid that drains into bowl. Gently press cheese to remove excess liquid.

Prepare Graham Crust; set aside. In a 1- to 1½-quart pan, combine gelatin and water; let stand for 5 minutes to soften gelatin, then stir over low heat until gelatin is dissolved.

Turn yogurt cheese out of strainer into a blender or food processor. Add gelatin mixture, cottage cheese, sugar, lime peel, and lime juice; whirl until smooth. Pour into Graham Crust, cover, and refrigerate until firm (at least 4 hours) or until next day.

To serve, top pie with berries. Makes 8 servings.

Graham Crust. In a 9-inch pie pan, mix 1⅓ cups **graham cracker crumbs**, 3 tablespoons **sugar,** and ⅓ cup **margarine** (melted). Press evenly over bottom and sides of pan. Bake in a 350° oven for 10 minutes.

Warm Gingerbread

Per serving:
278 *calories* (28% fat, 66% carbohydrates, 6% protein), 9 g *total fat* (2 g saturated), 46 g *carbohydrates*, 4 g *protein*, 35 mg *cholesterol*, 332 mg *sodium*

Preparation time: About 20 minutes

Baking time: About 25 minutes

A bowl of Beef & Pumpkin Soup (page 20), a leafy salad, and a big wedge of warm, spicy gingerbread add up to a satisfying midwinter meal. If you like, decorate the gingerbread with a snowy powdered-sugar pattern: place a doily on the uncut cake, then sift on a little sugar and carefully lift off the doily.

- ¼ **cup margarine, at room temperature**
- ¼ **cup granulated sugar**
- 1 **large egg, lightly beaten**
- ½ **cup light molasses**
- 1¼ **cups all-purpose flour**
- 1 **teaspoon baking soda**
- ¼ **teaspoon *each* ground nutmeg and salt**
- 1 **teaspoon ground ginger (or 1 tablespoon minced fresh ginger; or 3 tablespoons minced crystallized ginger)**
- ½ **cup hot water**
  About 1 tablespoon powdered sugar (optional)

In a medium-size bowl, beat margarine, granulated sugar, and egg until blended. Beat in molasses. In another bowl, stir together flour, baking soda, nutmeg, salt, and ginger; add to egg mixture alternately with hot water, stirring until smooth after each addition. Pour batter into a greased, floured 8- or 9-inch-round baking pan and spread evenly.

Bake gingerbread in a 350° oven until a wooden pick inserted in center comes out clean (about 25 minutes). Let cool in pan on a rack until just warm to the touch (about 15 minutes); then turn out onto a rack. Invert a serving plate over gingerbread; holding rack and plate together, invert both. Lift off rack.

Serve gingerbread warm or cool. Just before serving, place a doily or other pattern on gingerbread, if desired; then sift powdered sugar over it. Lift off doily. Makes 6 servings.

Summer Hazelnut Torte with Berries

Per serving:
230 **calories** *(27% fat, 64% carbohydrates, 9% protein), 7 g*
total fat (1 g saturated), 36 g **carbohydrates,** *5 g* **protein,**
35 mg **cholesterol,** *111 mg* **sodium**

Preparation time: About 20 minutes

Baking time: About 15 minutes

For a colorful summer dessert, spoon fresh berries over sugar-dusted wedges of nut-flavored sponge-cake. The cake tastes best if served the same day it's baked.

- ⅔ cup all-purpose flour
- ½ teaspoon baking powder
- 1 large egg
- 2 large egg whites
- ⅓ cup granulated sugar
- ⅛ teaspoon salt
- ½ teaspoon vanilla
- 2 teaspoons hazelnut oil or salad oil
  Berry Medley (recipe follows)
- 2 to 3 tablespoons hazelnut-flavored liqueur or amaretto
- ⅓ cup coarsely chopped hazelnuts
- 1 to 2 tablespoons powdered sugar

Sift flour and baking powder into a small bowl; set aside. In a large bowl, combine egg, egg whites, granulated sugar, and salt. Beat with an electric mixer at high speed until mixture is thick and almost tripled in volume (about 5 minutes). Beat in vanilla. Using a rubber spatula, gently fold in flour mixture until almost blended. Drizzle with oil; continue to fold gently just until all flour is mixed in. Spread batter in an oiled, flour-dusted 8-inch-round baking pan.

Bake in a 350° oven until top of cake is golden brown and a wooden pick inserted in center comes out clean (about 15 minutes). Let cake cool in pan for 5 minutes.

Carefully invert cake onto a rack and let stand until barely warm to the touch (about 10 minutes). Meanwhile, prepare Berry Medley.

To serve, transfer cake to a serving plate; drizzle with liqueur. Sprinkle with hazelnuts, then dust with powdered sugar. Cut cake into wedges; top each serving with Berry Medley. Makes 6 servings.

Berry Medley. In a medium-size bowl, lightly mix 1 cup *each* **raspberries** and **blackberries** with 1 to 2 tablespoons **sugar** and 2 teaspoons **kirsch** or lemon juice.

Orange Cake

Per serving:
233 **calories** *(28% fat, 66% carbohydrates, 6% protein), 7 g*
total fat (1 g saturated), 38 g **carbohydrates,** *3 g* **protein,**
53 mg **cholesterol,** *164 mg* **sodium**

Preparation time: About 40 minutes

Baking time: About 20 minutes

If you like oranges, you'll definitely want to add this moist cake to your file of favorites.

- 2 large eggs
- ½ cup sugar
- ¾ cup all-purpose flour
- 1½ teaspoons baking powder
- 2 tablespoons grated orange peel
- ¼ cup margarine, melted
  Orange Syrup (recipe follows)

In a large bowl, beat eggs and sugar with an electric mixer at high speed until thick and lemon colored. Add flour, baking powder, orange peel, and margarine; beat until well blended. Spread batter in a greased, floured 9-inch-round baking pan.

Bake in a 375° oven until cake just begins to pull from sides of pan and center springs back when lightly pressed (about 20 minutes).

Transfer cake (in pan) to a rack. Prepare Orange Syrup. Pierce cake all over with a fork. Slowly pour syrup over cake; let cool. Makes 8 servings.

Orange Syrup. In a 2-quart pan, mix ⅓ cup *each* **sugar** and **water** with 2 cups **orange juice.** Bring to a boil; boil, uncovered, until reduced to 1½ cups (about 10 minutes). Remove from heat; stir in 2 tablespoons **orange-flavored liqueur.** Use warm.

Summer Hazelnut Torte with Berries (recipe on facing page) is quick and easy to make—but it's a dazzling dessert. Top the cake with crunchy nuts and powdered sugar, then spoon a medley of fresh raspberries and blackberries over each wedge. Complete the occasion with a sparkling wine such as champagne or Asti spumante.

Appendix

For help in following a lowfat regime, consult the guides and references in this chapter. We begin with a glossary of terms commonly used by nutritionists, then move on to a review of the new Food Guide Pyramid—a chart that shows you how to structure a healthful daily diet. Next, we discuss several lowfat cooking techniques and offer a table of lower-fat substitutes for some typical recipe ingredients. On the following two pages, you'll find another guide for planning daily meals: the authoritative American Heart Association Diet. The chapter concludes with a discussion of the role of exercise in overall fitness, a chart of healthy weight limits for a range of ages and heights, tips on reading package labels for fat content, and four pages of tables providing nutritional information for a number of foods.

Glossary

Atherosclerosis. Process in which the lining of the arteries becomes coated with fatty substances. Blood vessels are narrowed and scarred by the deposits and may eventually become completely blocked. If the blockage occurs in an artery supplying blood to the heart, a heart attack results; if it occurs in an artery supplying blood to the brain, a stroke results.

Calorie. Measurement of the amount of energy produced when food is metabolized.

Carbohydrates. One of the three major nutrients supplying energy to the body (the other two are fat and protein). Providing fiber and about 4 calories per gram, carbohydrates are our most efficient source of energy, more readily available for use by the body than either protein or fat. They are essential for proper function of the brain and nervous system.

Carbohydrates are categorized as simple or complex. *Simple carbohydrates* are found in honey, syrups, jams, jellies, fruit, and fruit juices. *Complex carbohydrates,* classified as water soluble or water insoluble, are found in most fruits and vegetables and in foods such as whole grains, breads, and legumes.

Cholesterol. A waxy, fatlike substance essential to the structure of cell membranes and nerve sheaths and the production of vitamins and hormones. The liver manufactures sufficient cholesterol for the body's needs; dietary cholesterol comes from the foods we eat. Cholesterol is present in all foods of animal origin: meats, poultry, fish, eggs, and dairy products.

Both dietary cholesterol and the cholesterol synthesized in the body affect the amount of cholesterol circulating in the bloodstream. This amount, measured in milligrams per deciliter, is known as the *blood cholesterol level.*

Dietary fiber. The undigested portion of food. Found only in plants, dietary fiber is either soluble or insoluble. Some types of fiber may help lower blood cholesterol. (For more on fiber, see page 5.)

Fats. One of the three major nutrients supplying energy to the body (the other two are carbohydrates and protein). Providing about 9 calories per gram, fats play an important role in cell maintenance and vitamin absorption.

Fats are classified as saturated or unsaturated; unsaturated fats are further categorized as monounsaturated or polyunsaturated. *Saturated fats,* usually solid at room temperature, are typically found in foods of animal origin (such as meat and whole-milk dairy products) and in some vegetable products (palm and coconut oils, for example). Saturated fats tend to raise blood cholesterol.

Unsaturated fats, generally liquid at room temperature, most often come from plants and may help lower blood cholesterol. *Monounsaturated fats* include olive, peanut, and avocado oils; among *polyunsaturated fats* are corn, safflower, and sesame oils.

Hydrogenated fats such as margarine and vegetable shortening are polyunsaturated oils that have been converted to a more saturated form through the addition of hydrogen (a commercial process called hydrogenation). These fats tend to increase blood cholesterol.

Omega-3 fatty acids, a group of polyunsaturated fats found primarily in cold-water marine fish such as salmon and tuna, may help lower cholesterol levels.

Lipoproteins. Fat-protein molecules that carry cholesterol in the blood. *High-density lipoprotein* (HDL), known as "good cholesterol," may be responsible for carrying cholesterol away from cells and tissues back to the liver for elimination. It's assumed to protect against atherosclerosis. *Low-density lipoprotein* (LDL), often termed "bad cholesterol," may be responsible for depositing cholesterol on the artery walls. A higher LDL level is assumed to indicate a greater risk of atherosclerosis.

Protein. One of the three major nutrients supplying energy to the body (the other two are fat and carbohydrates). Protein provides about 4 calories per gram; it's made up of amino acids, substances essential for maintaining healthy muscles, bone, skin, and blood. Animal products provide *complete protein,* protein that contains all eight of the amino acids required for good health. Plant products (except soybeans) provide *incomplete protein,* supplying less than the full range of essential amino acids. You can usually correct such deficiencies by combining plant foods (by mixing grains with legumes, for example).

Triglycerides. The major component of fatty tissues, triglycerides are blood fats manufactured by the liver from excess dietary fats, carbohydrates, and alcohol. No direct relationship has been determined between levels of triglycerides and the risk of heart disease, but individuals with very high triglyceride counts may be advised to lose weight (if they are overweight) and to limit or avoid alcohol and concentrated sugars.

Food Guide Pyramid A Guide to Daily Food Choices

The pyramid below is a healthful daily eating plan that can help you choose a diet that's right for you. The plan calls for eating a variety of foods, both to provide required nutrients and to supply the calories necessary for maintaining a healthy weight. Because most Americans' diets are too high in fat—especially saturated fat—the plan focuses on fat reduction.

How the Pyramid Promotes a Good Diet

Using the pyramid will make it simpler for you to follow these modern dietary guidelines:

- Eat a variety of foods
- Maintain a healthy weight
- Choose a diet low in fat, saturated fat, and cholesterol

- Choose a diet with plenty of vegetables, fruits, and grain products
- Use sugars, salt, and sodium in moderation
- If you drink alcoholic beverages, do so in moderation

The Pyramid's Five Food Groups

The Food Guide Pyramid emphasizes foods from the five groups shown in the bottom three levels. Each of these groups provides some—but not all—of the nutrients you need every day. Foods in one group can't replace those in another. No single group is more important than another; for good health, you need them all.

The tip of the pyramid shows fats, oils, and sweets. These are foods such as salad dressings and oils,

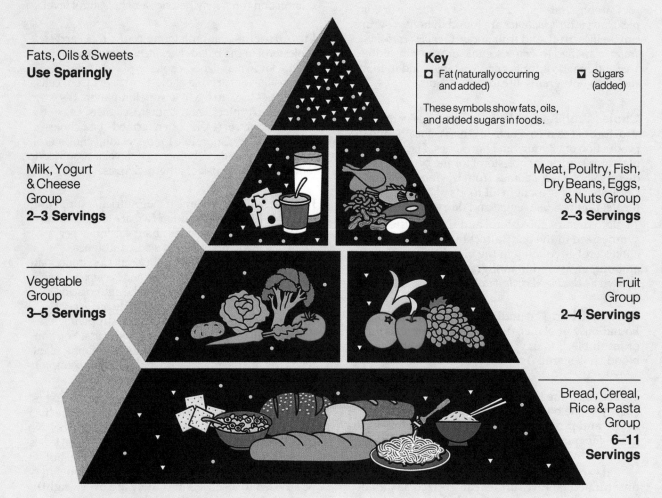

Fats, Oils & Sweets
Use Sparingly

Key
◻ Fat (naturally occurring and added)   ▾ Sugars (added)

These symbols show fats, oils, and added sugars in foods.

Milk, Yogurt & Cheese Group
2–3 Servings

Meat, Poultry, Fish, Dry Beans, Eggs, & Nuts Group
2–3 Servings

Vegetable Group
3–5 Servings

Fruit Group
2–4 Servings

Bread, Cereal, Rice & Pasta Group
6–11 Servings

Source: United States Department of Agriculture

cream, butter, margarine, sugars (corn syrup, honey, molasses, and brown, white, and raw sugar), soft drinks, candy, and sweet desserts. These foods provide calories and little else nutritionally, so most people should use them sparingly.

On the next level of the Food Guide Pyramid are two groups of foods that come largely from animals: milk, yogurt, and cheese; and meat, poultry, fish, dry beans, eggs, and nuts. These foods are important sources of protein, calcium, iron, and zinc.

The level above the base includes vegetables and fruits—foods that come from plants. Most people need to eat plenty of these foods for the vitamins, minerals, and fiber they supply.

At the base of the pyramid are breads, cereals, rice, and pasta—all foods from grains. In your daily meals, you need more servings of these than of any other foods.

Using the Pyramid

The pyramid states a range of servings for each food group. The number of servings you need depends on your calorie requirements—which in turn depend on your age, sex, size, and level of daily activity. However, almost everyone needs at least the lower number of servings in each range.

Nutritionists recommend that sedentary women and some older adults consume about 1,600 calories a day. Preschoolers should have the same variety of foods as older family members do, but may need less than 1,600 calories; they can simply eat smaller servings, but it's important that they have the equivalent of 2 cups of milk a day.

Most older children, teenage girls, active women, and sedentary men require about 2,200 calories; women who are pregnant or breastfeeding may need somewhat more. Teenage boys, many active men, and some very active women need as many as 2,800 calories daily.

What Is a Serving?

The amount of food that counts as a serving is listed below for typical foods in each group of the pyramid. If you eat a larger portion, count it as more than one serving.

Bread, Cereal, Rice & Pasta Group: 1 slice of bread; 1 ounce of ready-to-eat cereal; ½ cup of cooked cereal, rice, or pasta

Vegetable Group: 1 cup of raw leafy vegetables; ½ cup of other vegetables, cooked or chopped raw; ¾ cup of vegetable juice

Fruit Group: 1 medium-size apple, banana, or orange; ½ cup of chopped, cooked, or canned fruit; ¾ cup of fruit juice

Milk, Yogurt & Cheese Group: 1 cup of milk or yogurt; 1½ ounces of natural cheese; 2 ounces of process cheese

Meat, Poultry, Fish, Dry Beans, Eggs & Nuts Group: 2 to 3 ounces of cooked lean meat, poultry, or fish; one egg, ½ cup of cooked dry beans, or 2 tablespoons of peanut butter count as 1 ounce of lean meat

Sample Daily Diets at Three Calorie Levels

	Lower (about 1,600)	Moderate (about 2,200)	High (about 2,800)
Bread group servings	6	9	11
Vegetable group servings	3	4	5
Fruit group servings	2	3	4
Milk group servings	2–3*	2–3*	2–3*
Meat group (ounces)**	5	6	7
Total fat (grams)	53	73	93
Total added sugars (teaspoons)	6	12	18

*Women who are pregnant or breastfeeding, teenagers, and young adults to age 24 need 3 servings.

** Meat group amounts are in total ounces.

Fat-lowering Cooking Techniques

Learning a few basic techniques for minimizing the butter, margarine, or oil used in cooking can help you prepare leaner versions of your favorite recipes. As substitutes for French fries and whipped cream—two of the high-fat foods listed on page 101—we also include a pair of recipes: a surprisingly simple dessert topping and some crisp oven-fried potatoes to serve with lean burgers or grilled meats and poultry.

■ **Braise-deglaze.** Many recipes for soups, stews, and sauces begin with chopped vegetables (such as onions, garlic, carrots, celery, and bell peppers) cooked in butter or oil to develop a flavor base. You can also achieve rich, satisfying flavor using fat-free liquids—and little or no actual fat. For example, if a recipe calls for 3 to 4 tablespoons fat, omit it altogether. Instead, put the vegetables in the specified cooking pan, then almost cover them with a liquid that will complement the flavor of the finished dish—broth, dry wine, or just plain water. If you're not using a nonstick pan, coat the pan with vegetable oil cooking spray before adding the vegetables; or stir ½ to 1 teaspoon unsaturated vegetable oil into the vegetables before pouring in the liquid.

Boil over high or medium-high heat, uncovered, stirring occasionally, until the liquid cooks away and the vegetables begin to brown and stick to the pan. Then add more liquid, 2 tablespoons at a time, stirring to release the browned bits from the pan (the vegetables will absorb the brown color). Repeat this reduction and deglazing process until the color is rich and appealing; watch closely to prevent scorching. Then proceed as the recipe directs.

Many of the recipes in this book use the braising-deglazing technique; examples include Italian Sausage Soup (page 20) and Braised Chicken with Green Chile Sauce (page 48).

■ **Oven braise-deglaze.** You can braise and deglaze in the oven as well as on top of the range. Follow the directions above, but use a shallow rimmed baking pan in a 450° oven; start with ¼ cup liquid, then pour in additional liquid in ¼-cup portions. The initial reduction will take about 15 minutes.

■ **Oven-fry.** Small pieces of food (such as meatballs, cut-up chicken or meat, or sliced vegetables), arranged in a single layer and lightly coated with vegetable oil (or olive oil) cooking spray, brown well in a hot oven—400° to 500°, depending on the food. Be sure to leave enough space between the pieces to let moisture evaporate quickly. Norwegian Meatballs (page 12) use this technique. Or try the following potato treat when you crave French fries.

Spicy Baked Potato Sticks. Scrub 3 or 4 small **russet potatoes** (about 1½ lbs. *total*), but do not peel. Cut each potato into 4 to 8 wedges. Spray a shallow rimmed baking pan with **olive oil cooking spray.** Place potatoes in pan, skin sides down, in a single layer; spray with cooking spray. Mix ½ teaspoon **ground cumin** and ⅛ teaspoon **ground red pepper** (cayenne); sprinkle over potatoes. Bake, uncovered, in a 400° oven until potatoes are brown and tender when pierced (about 1 hour). Season to taste with **salt,** if desired. Makes 4 servings.

Per serving: 142 calories (5% fat, 86% carbohydrates, 9% protein), 1 g total fat (0 g saturated), 31 g carbohydrates, 3 g protein, 0 mg cholesterol, 14 mg sodium

■ **Use more egg whites** and fewer whole eggs or egg yolks. Egg whites serve much the same function as whole eggs in many recipes, and omitting all or most of the yolks reduces fat, calories, and cholesterol. Summer Hazelnut Torte with Berries (page 94) uses this technique.

■ **Choose reduced-fat, lowfat, or nonfat dairy products.** Lower-fat milk, yogurt, cheese, and sour cream are all widely sold. In cream sauces and in mashed potatoes or other puréed vegetables, try rich-tasting evaporated skim milk—or use it in this frothy dessert topping.

Lowfat Whipped Topping. Pour ½ cup **evaporated skim milk** into bowl of an electric mixer. Cover bowl; then refrigerate milk and beaters for 1 hour. Beat chilled milk at high speed until fluffy (30 seconds to 1 minute). Add 1 tablespoon **powdered sugar** and ¼ teaspoon **vanilla;** continue to beat until mixture holds soft peaks. Serve immediately. Makes 6 to 8 servings.

Per serving: 19 calories (0% fat, 70% carbohydrates, 30% protein), 0 g total fat (0 g saturated), 3 g carbohydrates, 1 g protein, 1 mg cholesterol, 21 mg sodium

■ **Fill in with water.** You can give sauces a velvety quality without using much fat; just replace some or all of the butter, margarine, or oil with slightly thickened water or other liquid (as appropriate to the dish). For each cup of liquid, use 1 tablespoon flour for a thin sauce, 2 tablespoons for a medium sauce, and 3 to 4 tablespoons for a thick sauce. If you use cornstarch, arrowroot, or potato starch, you'll need just half these amounts of starch for the same thickening effect after cooking.

Substitutions for Reducing Fat & Cholesterol

Instead of	Choose
Bacon	Canadian bacon
Beef, regular ground	Extra-lean ground beef or ground skinned turkey breast (or half of each)
Butter	Polyunsaturated margarine with liquid oil listed as the first ingredient
Buttermilk	For each cup, use 1 tablespoon lemon juice or distilled white vinegar plus enough nonfat milk to equal 1 cup; or use nonfat or lowfat buttermilk
Cheese	Lowfat cheeses such as part-skim mozzarella and part-skim ricotta. Use nonfat or lowfat cottage cheese; use Romano or Parmesan in small quantities
Chicken, whole	Skinned chicken breast
Chocolate, unsweetened	For each ounce, use 3 tablespoons unsweetened cocoa plus 1 tablespoon salad oil
Cream	Evaporated skim milk
Cream, whipped	Lowfat Whipped Topping (page 100)
Eggs	For every 2 whole eggs, use 1 egg plus 2 egg whites
French-fried potatoes	Spicy Baked Potato Sticks (page 100)
Ice cream	Frozen nonfat or lowfat yogurt, fruit ices, and sherbets
Mayonnaise	Reduced-calorie mayonnaise or half mayonnaise and half plain nonfat yogurt
Milk, whole	Nonfat milk
Peanuts	Pretzels
Potato chips	Air-popped popcorn (spray with vegetable oil cooking spray so seasonings such as chili powder or cinnamon will adhere)
Salad dressings	Lowfat bottled dressings or homemade dressings
Shortening, solid	Unsaturated vegetable oil
Sour cream	Plain nonfat or lowfat yogurt or reduced-fat sour cream
Tuna or sardines packed in oil	Tuna or sardines packed in water

The American Heart Association Diet

Meat, Poultry & Fish

High in Protein, B Vitamins, and Iron and Other Minerals

Servings per day: No more than 6 oz. cooked lean meat, poultry and fish
Serving size: 3 oz. cooked (4 oz. raw) lean meat, poultry or fish

Here are some examples to help you judge serving sizes of meat, poultry and fish. A 3-ounce portion equals:

- the size of a deck of playing cards
- 2 thin slices of lean roast beef (each slice 3"x3"x¼")
- ½ of a chicken breast or a chicken leg with thigh (without skin)
- ¾ cup of flaked fish

Choose from:

Fish—fresh, frozen, canned in water (or rinsed)
*Shellfish
Chicken (without skin)
Cornish hen (without skin)
Turkey (without skin)
Turkey, ground
**Lean beef (from the round, sirloin, loin)
Lean or extra lean ground beef
+Lean ham
Lean pork (tenderloin, loin chop)
Lamb (except rib)
Veal (except commercially ground)
++Wild game—rabbit, venison, pheasant, duck (without skin)

- Organ meats are very high in cholesterol. However, liver is rich in iron and vitamins and a small serving (3 ounces) is okay about once a month.
- Trim off all the fat before cooking meat. Drain or skim off fat from cooked meats before using juices in stews, soups, gravies, etc.
- Remove the skin and fat under the skin from poultry pieces before cooking. If you're roasting a whole chicken or turkey, leave the skin on to keep the bird from getting too dry while roasting. Then remove the skin before carving and serving the meat.
- Select whole turkeys that have not been injected with fats or broths.
- Frozen dinners and entrées may also fit into the plan. Look for those that are made specially for low-fat, low-cholesterol, low-sodium diets.
- One cup serving of cooked beans, peas or lentils, or 3 ounces of soybean curd (tofu), can replace a 3 ounce serving of meat, poultry or fish

Eggs

High in Protein, B Vitamins, and Iron and Other Minerals

Servings per week: 3 to 4 egg yolks a week may be eaten (egg whites are not limited)

- Because of their cholesterol content (213 mg per yolk), limit your whole eggs and egg yolks to no more than 3 to 4 per week. Be sure to count any egg yolks used in cooking and in store-bought foods in your total for the week.
- Use two egg whites, or one egg white plus 2 teaspoons of unsaturated oil, in place of one whole egg in cooking. You can also use cholesterol-free commercial egg substitutes.
- Eat only *cooked* eggs and egg whites—not raw.

Vegetables & Fruits

High in Vitamins, Minerals and Fiber; Low in Fat, Calories and Sodium . . . Contains *no* Cholesterol

Servings per day: 5 or more
Serving size: 1 medium size piece of fruit or ½ cup fruit juice ½–1 cup cooked or raw vegetables

Choose from:

All vegetables and fruits except coconut. Olives and avocados should be counted as fats (see Fats & Oils section). Starchy vegetables are listed with Breads, Cereals, Pasta & Starchy Vegetables because they are similar in calories per serving to the other foods in that group.

- Enjoy plenty of fruits and vegetables. If you are watching your weight, these foods will give you vitamins, minerals and fiber with few calories. Be sure to include sources rich in vitamin C and vitamin A.
- Check the labels for sodium content of canned vegetables.

Milk Products

High in Protein, Calcium, Phosphorus, Niacin, Riboflavin, Vitamins A and D

Servings per day: 2 or more for adults over 24 years and children 2–10 years; 3–4 for ages 11–24 and women who are pregnant or breastfeeding
Serving size: 1 cup skim, ½% or 1% fat milk 1 cup nonfat or low-fat yogurt 1 oz. low-fat cheese or ½ cup low-fat cottage cheese

Choose from:

Milk products with 0–1% fat:
skim milk
½–1% fat milk
nonfat or low-fat dry milk powder
evaporated skim milk
buttermilk made from skim or 1% fat milk
nonfat or low-fat yogurt
drinks made with skim or 1% fat milk and cocoa (or other low-fat drink powders)
Low-fat cheeses:
dry-curd, skim or low-fat cottage cheese
natural or processed cheeses with no more than 5 grams of fat per ounce

- Skim, ½% fat and 1% fat milk all provide the same nutrients as whole milk and 2% fat milk. But they are much lower in fat, saturated fatty acids, cholesterol and calories.
- If you're used to whole milk products, you may find it easier to make the change slowly to lower fat foods. Try 2% fat milk first. Then when you're used to that, move to 1% fat milk. That will make it much easier if you decide to change to skim milk.

---

*Shrimp and crayfish are higher in cholesterol than most other types of fish, but lower in fat and cholesterol than most meats and poultry.

**Buy "choice" or "select" grades of beef rather than "prime."

+Ham and Canadian bacon are higher in sodium than other meats.

++Domesticated versions of game (duck and goose) are not as lean as wild game.

Breads, Cereals, Pasta & Starchy Vegetables

Low in Fat and Cholesterol; High in B Vitamins, Iron and Fiber

Servings per day: 6 or more
Serving size: 1 slice bread
¼ cup nugget or bud-type cereal
½ cup hot cereal
1 cup flaked cereal
1 cup cooked rice or pasta
¼–½ cup starchy vegetables
1 cup low-fat soup

Choose from:
Breads and rolls
  wheat, rye, raisin or white bread
  English muffins
  frankfurter and hamburger buns
  water (not egg) bagels
  pita bread
  tortillas (not fried)
*Crackers and snacks
  animal, graham, rye crackers
  soda, saltine, oyster crackers
  matzo
  fig bar, ginger snap, molasses cookies
  bread sticks, melba toast
  rusks, flat bread
  pretzels (unsalted)
  popcorn (see "Fats & Oils" for preparation)
**Quick breads
  homemade using margarine or oils low in saturated fatty acids, skim or 1% fat milk, and egg whites or egg substitutes (or egg yolks within limits)
  biscuits, muffins, cornbread
  fruit breads, soft rolls
  pancakes, French toast, waffles
+Hot or cold cereals
  all kinds (granola-type may be high in fat or saturated fatty acids)
+Rice and pasta
  all kinds (pasta made without egg yolk)
Starchy vegetables
  potatoes, corn
  lima beans, green peas
  winter squash
  yams, sweet potatoes
++Soups
  chicken noodle
  tomato-based seafood chowders
  minestrone
  onion
  split pea

*Many kinds of crackers and snacks are now available with no added salt or unsalted tops. Some are high in saturated fatty acids, so read the labels.

**If you use any egg yolks in cooking quick breads, be sure to count them in your daily allowance.

+Cereals, pasta and rice cooked without salt are lower in sodium than instant or ready-to-eat types of these foods.

++Most soups are high in sodium and some are high in fat. When buying soups, read labels and choose those low in sodium and fat. You can also make your own soups and control both sodium and fat.

Fats & Oils

Some of these foods are high in vitamins A or E, but all are high in fat and calories.

Servings per day: No more than a total of 5–8, depending on your caloric needs
Serving size: 1 tsp. vegetable oil or regular margarine
2 tsp. diet margarine
1 Tbsp. salad dressing
2 tsp. mayonnaise or peanut butter
3 tsp. seeds or nuts
⅛ of medium avocado
10 small or 5 large olives

Choose from:
Vegetable oils and margarines with no more than 2 grams of saturated fatty acids per tablespoon—canola, corn, olive, safflower, sesame, soybean, sunflower. Salad dressings and mayonnaise with no more than 1 gram of saturated fatty acids per tablespoon.

- Use fats and oils sparingly—and use the ones lowest in saturated fatty acids and cholesterol.

- Use hydrogenated shortenings sparingly and choose those made from vegetable fat. They are lower in saturated fatty acids than those made from animal/vegetable fat blends.

- Use cooking styles that add little or no fat to food, and ask for them when eating out.

- Remember to count the "hidden fat" in bakery and snack foods as well as the fats used in cooking and on vegetables and breads.

- Remember that although coconut oil, palm oil and palm kernel oil are vegetable oils and have no cholesterol, they are high in saturated fatty acids. *Read food labels carefully.*

Desserts

Choose:
Desserts low in saturated fatty acids, cholesterol and calories. For a special treat, share a dessert portion with someone.

First choices (low in fat and saturated fatty acids):

  Fruit—fresh, frozen, canned or dried
  Low-fat yogurt with fruit
  Crackers and cookies (as listed in the Breads section)
  Angel food cake
  Frozen low-fat or nonfat yogurt
  Sherbet or ice milk
  Flavored gelatin
  Water ices or sorbets

Special occasions only (higher in fat and calories):

Homemade desserts (cakes, pies, cookies, puddings)—made with margarine or oils low in saturated fatty acids, skim or 1% fat milk, and egg whites or egg substitutes (or egg yolks within limits).

Store-bought desserts—many are now made with unsaturated oils and are either low-fat or nonfat. Be sure to read ingredient lists.

Snacks

Choose snacks from other food groups, such as:
Fruits and juices
Raw vegetables and low-fat dips
Low-fat cookies
Low-fat crackers
Plain unsalted popcorn
Unsalted pretzels
Hard candy, gum drops
Sugar, syrup, honey, jam, jelly, marmalade (as spreads)

Beverages

First choices:
Fruit or vegetable juice, coffee, tea, plain or flavored mineral water, low-sodium broth and low-sodium bouillon

Other choices:
Fruit punches, carbonated soft drinks
Alcoholic beverages—If you drink them, do so in moderation. Have no more than two drinks per day of wine, beer or liquor, and only when caloric limits allow. Here are the amounts to count as *one* drink (½ ounce pure alcohol):

  12 oz. beer
  1½ oz. 80 proof spirits (bourbon, gin, rum, Scotch, tequila, vodka, whiskey)
  1 oz. 100 proof spirits
  4 oz. wine (red, white, rosé)
If you don't drink, don't start!

Reproduced with permission
© *The American Heart Association Diet*
American Heart Association

Exercising for Fitness

Keeping fit involves more than putting the right things into your body; the energy you expend affects your health, too. That's why exercise is so important. Of course, any activity at any level burns calories; but to become truly fit, you need to work at your endurance level, or target heart rate, regularly.

Why be fit? Study after study has shown that physically active people have more stamina and manage their weight better than sedentary people. Other benefits include increased HDL ("good cholesterol"), decreased incidence of heart disease, reduced blood pressure, and buildup of bone mass (helpful in minimizing the debilitating effects of osteoporosis).

Happily, you don't have to be a serious athlete to reap the rewards of exercise. In fact, scientific evidence shows that people who move just one level up from sedentary—by taking a brisk walk for only 30 to 60 minutes a day—make substantial gains on the road to fitness. To start, all you need to do is get moving; then keep it up, gently pushing yourself to higher levels.

It's easy to be fit. Various health organizations recommend that every person burn *at least 300 calories daily* in some form of physical activity. An average (150-lb.) adult walking at a brisk pace (3 to 3.5 miles per hour) for an hour will burn about 300 calories; so will a person who does half an hour of vigorous aerobic dancing or an hour of mowing, weeding, or raking in the yard.

What can you do if you don't have an hour to devote to exercise every day? Look for creative ways to incorporate activity into your regular schedule: walk up stairs instead of using elevators; take a walk during lunch; do calisthenics while watching the evening news.

How do you know when you're fit? Standard signs of fitness include improved cardiovascular capacity, muscle strength and endurance, flexibility, and a favorable balance of lean and fat body composition. Remember, though, that individual differences mean that each person feels fit at a different level. Whatever that point is for you, exercise is one of the best ways to get there.

The most important component of physical fitness is *improved cardiovascular capacity*, or the ability to engage in a vigorous activity over an extended period of time. This type of conditioning is gained through regular, vigorous aerobic exercise—that is, exercise that extends over a period of more than a few minutes and stresses the cardiovascular system to increase oxygen delivery to the muscles. Such exercise includes brisk walking, jogging, skiing, and lap swimming.

To build *muscular strength*, the force exerted by a muscle group, many people turn to weight lifting, which expends energy in short, anaerobic bursts. Repeated muscular contractions, such as push-ups, build *muscular endurance*—the ability to perform stop-and-start activities over and over.

Flexibility is the ability of joints to move through their full range of motion; it's built through gentle, static stretching of muscle groups. *Proper body composition* is achieved through a balance of exercise and a lowfat, high-carbohydrate diet (to find out how many calories you should eat in a day, see page 99).

Determining your target heart rate. To gain optimum benefits from aerobic exercise, you need to work at endurance level—that is, at your target heart rate—for at least 20 minutes a minimum of three times a week.

The simplest way to calculate target heart rate is to subtract your age from 220, then multiply by both 60% and 80%; your target rate per minute should fall between the two numbers.

Here's a sample calculation for a 45-year-old person:

$$220 - 45 = 175$$
$$60\% \text{ of } 175 = 105 \ (.6 \times 175)$$
$$80\% \text{ of } 175 = 140 \ (.8 \times 175)$$

In this case, the target heart rate should be between 105 and 140 beats per minute.

Target heart rates for some other ages are as follows:

Age 20: 120 to 160 beats per minute

Age 25: 117 to 156 beats per minute

Age 30: 114 to 152 beats per minute

Age 35: 111 to 148 beats per minute

Age 40: 108 to 144 beats per minute

Age 50: 102 to 136 beats per minute

Age 55: 99 to 132 beats per minute

Age 60: 96 to 128 beats per minute

Age 65: 93 to 124 beats per minute

To find out if you're reaching your target heart rate, work out for at least 10 minutes. Stop and count your pulse for 10 seconds; then multiply this number by 6 to calculate your heart rate per minute. If the number is less than your target rate, increase your pace; if it's above your target rate, slow down.

When you're beginning an exercise program, work at the lower target heart rate figure; as your fitness increases, gradually work up to the higher level. Each time you work out, be sure to warm up first for a few minutes by jogging in place or doing your planned exercise at a slower pace.

After exercising, when your muscles are warmed and flexible, do some gentle stretching to cool down; don't bounce while stretching. Never come to a complete stop right after finishing a vigorous exercise; always taper off slowly.

Exercise more, eat more. As you burn calories through exercise, you can consume more calories. This translates to eating more and, if you're choosing a healthy diet, to extra nutritional benefits: when you eat more, you take in nutrients in greater quantities. For example, an average inactive 45-year-old woman who needs 800 milligrams of calcium and 15 milligrams of iron each day may not be meeting those requirements with her current caloric intake. But if the same woman were to start exercising enough to burn 300 calories per day, she could add another 300 calories of calcium- and iron-rich foods to her daily diet without gaining weight.

Go do it! Exercise is good for you, and that's the best reason to do it. If you'd like to lose weight, you'll probably find it easier to increase your caloric expenditure through exercise than to decrease your intake. Moreover, you'll feel a lot better.

If an exercise program is to be successful, however, it has to be fun and adapted to your needs and lifestyle. Don't decide on a form of exercise that's inconvenient, too costly for you, or easily called off because of other circumstances. Choose something you enjoy and can do on a regular basis— if exercise is a hassle, it won't get done. And if it doesn't get done, you won't reap the benefits of fitness.

A word of warning. If you're just starting an exercise program, begin slowly. Select the proper exercise for your capacity, and always use common sense: if something you're doing hurts, back off. *Consult your physician before beginning any exercise regimen.*

What Is a Healthy Weight for You?

The guidelines below will help you judge if your weight is within the range suggested for persons of your age and height. Note that the table shows higher weights for people 35 years and above than for younger adults; recent research indicates that gaining a little extra weight with age does not significantly increase health risks.

Suggested Weights for Adults

Height (without shoes)	Weight in pounds* (without clothes)		Height (without shoes)	Weight in pounds* (without clothes)	
	19 to 34 years	35 years and over		19 to 34 years	35 years and over
5'0"	97–128	108–138	5'10"	132–174	146–188
5'1"	101–132	111–143	5'11"	136–179	151–194
5'2"	104–137	115–148	6'0"	140–184	155–199
5'3"	107–141	119–152	6'1"	144–189	159–205
5'4"	111–146	122–157	6'2"	148–195	164–210
5'5"	114–150	126–162	6'3"	152–200	168–216
5'6"	118–155	130–167	6'4"	156–205	173–222
5'7"	121–160	134–172	6'5"	160–211	177–228
5'8"	125–164	138–178	6'6"	164–216	182–234
5'9"	129–169	142–183			

The higher weights in the ranges generally apply to men, who tend to have more muscle and bone; the lower weights more often apply to women, who have less muscle and bone.
Source: Dietary Guidelines for Americans, Third Edition, 1990, U.S. Department of Agriculture, U.S. Department of Health and Human Services.

How to Read Food Labels

No cholesterol! Low fat! These claims are made for many foods. How do you verify and interpret such statements? When you buy any canned or packaged food, it pays to understand nutrition labels—especially when it comes to calculating the percentage of calories provided by fat.

Today's laws require that nutritional information be provided for any food to which nutrients have been added or for which health claims are made. Under new regulations, expected to be in place by 1994 at the latest, this information will be mandatory for most processed foods; eventually, you may also find such labeling on packages of fresh, unprocessed meat and poultry.

The information is given in a standard form. The serving size and servings per container are listed, followed by the calorie, protein, carbohydrate, and fat content per serving. Amounts of sodium, cholesterol, and saturated and unsaturated fat may or may not be stated. Once the new regulations are in force, serving sizes will be more realistic—and they'll be standardized, so that similar products will suggest the same quantity of food per serving. The new nutrition labels will also give information on calories from fat, grams of saturated fat, and dietary fiber.

Current nutrition labels show the percentage of the U.S. Recommended Daily Allowances for protein, vitamins, and minerals provided by one serving. Keep in mind that these recommended intakes may also change as nutritional needs are studied further.

Finally, the ingredients are listed in descending order by weight.

Determining the calorie breakdown. Until labels are required to give a calorie breakdown, you can calculate this information yourself using a simple formula. Look at the following sample label information, similar to that you might find on a snack food package.

> *Nutrition Information Per Serving:*
> *Serving size: 1 oz.*
> *Servings per container: 4*
> *Calories: 160*
> *Protein (grams): 3*
> *Carbohydrates (grams): 12*
> *Fat (grams): 11*
> *Sodium (milligrams): 10*
> *Cholesterol (milligrams): 0*

To calculate the percentage of calories from fat in any food, multiply the number of grams of fat per serving by 9. In our example, $11 \times 9 = 99$. Divide the fat calories by the total calories: $99 \div 160 = 0.62$. Then multiply this figure by 100 to find the percent: $0.62 \times 100 = 62\%$. Keep in mind that the American Heart Association (AHA) recommends that no more than 30% of your daily calories come from fat.

The AHA also recommends that about 55% of the day's calories come from carbohydrates. To determine carbohydrate calories, multiply the grams of carbohydrates per serving by 4; in our example, $12 \times 4 = 48$. Then divide your answer by the total calories and multiply by 100 to get the percentage. Thus, $48 \div 160 = 0.30$; $0.30 \times 100 = 30\%$. You can use the same method to determine the percent of protein calories: protein, like carbohydrates, provides about 4 calories per gram.

What you've learned from our sample label, then, is that the product, though cholesterol-free, contains about 62% fat and 30% carbohydrates—just about the reverse of the situation you'd like to see for daily calorie intake. You'd be better off choosing a snack that is not only low in cholesterol, but also lower in fat and higher in carbohydrates.

NOTE: The 4-9-4 formula—4 calories per gram of protein, 9 calories per gram of fat, and 4 calories per gram of carbohydrates—is a very useful approximation, but it is not exact. A detailed nutritional analysis must also account for other factors: non-nutritive fiber in some carbohydrates, for example, and calories from alcohol (which occurs naturally in some fresh fruits). For this reason, when you check our data with the 4-9-4 formula, the numbers may not always agree precisely.

Using the ingredient list. You can read the ingredient list to confirm claims made about a food. For instance, if no ingredients from animal sources are mentioned, the food can be accurately described as cholesterol-free. (However, it may still be high in saturated fats, which tend to raise blood cholesterol.)

You can also use the list in other ways. If you want to limit your intake of saturated fat, for example, choose a margarine that lists liquid oil before partially hydrogenated oil; that way, you'll be getting more unsaturated fat than saturated.

Be aware that manufacturers are permitted to list fats with the explanation "contains one or more of the following." If you're trying to avoid saturated fat, you may decide not to purchase a product that includes in its list of ingredients a statement such as "contains one or more of the following: soybean and/or palm kernel oil." Such a statement doesn't tell you whether the food contains saturated, unsaturated, or both kinds of fat.

Food Tables

Food/Portion	Calories	Total Fat (grams)	Saturated Fat (grams)	Protein (grams)	Carbohydrates (grams)	Cholesterol (milligrams)
POULTRY, SEAFOOD & MEATS						
Poultry						
Chicken breast, meat and skin, roasted (3½ oz.)	195	8	2	30	0	83
Chicken breast, meat only, roasted (3½ oz.)	164	4	1	31	0	84
Chicken thigh, meat and skin, roasted (3½ oz.)	245	15	4	25	0	92
Chicken thigh, meat only, roasted (3½ oz.)	207	11	3	26	0	94
Chicken liver, simmered (3½ oz.)	156	5	2	24	0	626
Turkey, light meat, meat and skin, roasted (3½ oz.)	197	8	2	29	0	76
Turkey, light meat, meat only, roasted (3½ oz.)	153	3	1	30	0	68
Turkey, dark meat, meat and skin, roasted (3½ oz.)	221	12	3	27	0	89
Turkey, dark meat, meat only, roasted (3½ oz.)	184	7	2	28	0	87
Turkey, ground, cooked (3½ oz.)	227	14	4	24	0	68
Turkey, ground, skinned breast meat, cooked (3½ oz.)	153	3	1	30	0	68
Duck, meat and skin, roasted (3½ oz.)	334	28	10	19	0	83
Duck, meat only, roasted (3½ oz.)	189	7	2	29	0	88
Finfish						
Cod, Atlantic, cooked, dry heat (3½ oz.)	104	*	*	23	0	55
Flounder, cooked, dry heat (3½ oz.)	116	2	*	24	0	67
Halibut, cooked, dry heat (3½ oz.)	139	3	*	26	0	41
Mackerel, cooked, dry heat (3½ oz.)	260	18	4	24	0	74
Redfish, cooked, dry heat (3½ oz.)	120	2	*	24	0	55
Salmon, sockeye, grilled (3½ oz.)	216	11	2	27	0	87
Sea bass, cooked, dry heat (3½ oz.)	123	3	*	23	0	53
Snapper, cooked, dry heat (3½ oz.)	127	2	*	26	0	47
Swordfish, cooked, dry heat (3½ oz.)	154	5	1	25	0	50
Trout, rainbow, cooked, dry heat (3½ oz.)	150	4	*	26	0	72
Tuna, white, canned in oil, drained (3½ oz.)	185	8	n/a	26	0	31
Tuna, white, canned in water, drained (3½ oz.)	135	2	*	26	0	42
Shellfish						
Clams, cooked, moist heat (3½ oz.)	147	2	*	25	0	66
Crab, Alaskan king, cooked, moist heat (3½ oz.)	96	2	*	19	0	53
Lobster, cooked, moist heat (3½ oz.)	97	*	*	20	0	71
Oysters, raw (3½ oz.)	68	2	*	7	0	55
Scallops, raw (3½ oz.)	87	*	*	17	0	33
Shrimp, cooked, moist heat (3½ oz.)	98	1	*	21	0	193
Beef						
Flank steak, lean only, broiled (3½ oz.)	205	10	4	27	0	66
Porterhouse, broiled (3½ oz.)	303	22	9	25	0	82
Prime rib, cooked (3½ oz.)	355	29	12	22	0	83
Round steak, lean only, broiled (3½ oz.)	190	7	3	29	0	77
Tenderloin, lean only, broiled (3½ oz.)	209	10	4	28	0	83
Ground, extra-lean, broiled (3½ oz.)	254	16	6	25	0	83
Ground, lean, broiled (3½ oz.)	270	18	7	25	0	86
Ground, regular, broiled (3½ oz.)	287	21	8	24	0	89
Liver, braised (3½ oz.)	160	5	2	24	0	386
Veal						
Ground, cooked (3½ oz.)	171	8	3	24	0	102
Loin chop, lean only, braised (3½ oz.)	224	9	3	33	0	124

* Contains less than 1 gram

Food/Portion	Calories	Total Fat (grams)	Saturated Fat (grams)	Protein (grams)	Carbohydrates (grams)	Cholesterol (milligrams)
Lamb						
Leg, shank portion, lean only, roasted (3½ oz.)	179	7	2	28	0	86
Loin chops, lean only, broiled (3½ oz.)	214	10	3	30	0	94
Rack rib, roasted (3½ oz.)	356	30	13	21	0	96
Pork						
Bacon, pan-fried (3½ oz.)	572	49	17	30	0	84
Canadian bacon, grilled (3½ oz.)	184	8	3	24	0	58
Center loin, broiled (3½ oz.)	314	22	8	27	0	96
Shoulder, roasted (3½ oz.)	323	25	9	22	0	95
Tenderloin, roasted (3½ oz.)	165	5	2	29	0	92
Ham, boneless, canned, roasted (3½ oz.)	226	15	5	21	0	62
Spareribs, braised (3½ oz.)	394	30	12	29	0	120
FRUIT						
Apple (1 med.)	81	*	*	*	21	0
Apricots, dried (8 halves)	67	*	*	1	17	0
Avocado (1 med.)	324	31	5	4	15	0
Banana (1 med.)	105	*	*	1	27	0
Cantaloupe (½ cup)	28	*	*	*	7	0
Cherries, sweet (10 large)	49	*	*	*	11	0
Dates, dried (2)	46	*	*	*	12	0
Grapefruit (½ grapefruit)	38	*	*	*	10	0
Grapes, seedless (½ cup)	57	*	*	*	14	0
Orange, peeled (1 med.)	69	*	*	1	17	0
Peach (1 med.)	56	*	*	*	15	0
Pear (1 med.)	98	*	*	*	25	0
Pineapple, fresh (½ cup)	38	*	*	*	10	0
Plum (1 med.)	36	*	*	*	9	0
Prunes, dried (3)	60	*	*	*	16	0
Raisins (2 tbsp.)	54	*	*	*	14	0
Raspberries (½ cup)	30	*	*	*	7	0
Strawberries (½ cup)	23	*	*	*	5	0
Watermelon (½ cup)	26	*	*	*	6	0
VEGETABLES						
Artichokes, globe, cooked (1 med.)	53	*	*	3	12	0
Asparagus, fresh, cooked (½ cup)	23	*	*	2	4	0
Beans, green, fresh, cooked (½ cup)	22	*	*	1	5	0
Beans, lima, large dry, cooked (½ cup)	108	*	*	7	20	0
Broccoli, fresh, cooked (½ cup)	23	*	*	2	4	0
Cabbage, green, raw, shredded (½ cup)	8	*	*	*	2	0
Carrots, fresh, raw (½ cup)	24	*	*	*	6	0
Corn, fresh, cooked (½ cup)	89	1	*	3	21	0
Lettuce, green leaf (½ cup)	5	*	*	*	*	0
Mushrooms, fresh, raw (½ cup)	9	*	*	*	2	0
Peas, green, frozen, cooked (½ cup)	62	*	*	4	11	0
Pepper, bell, chopped (½ cup)	13	*	*	*	3	0
Potato, baked with skin (1 med.)	220	*	*	5	51	0
Potato, boiled, peeled (½ cup)	67	*	*	1	16	0
Potato, sweet, baked in skin, peeled (1 med.)	117	*	*	2	28	0
Spinach, fresh, raw (½ cup)	6	*	*	*	*	0
Squash, summer, fresh, cooked (½ cup)	18	*	*	*	4	0
Squash, winter, fresh, cooked (½ cup)	40	*	*	*	9	0
Tomatoes, fresh (½ cup)	17	*	*	*	4	0

* Contains less than 1 gram

Food/Portion	Calories	Total Fat (grams)	Saturated Fat (grams)	Monounsaturated Fat (grams)	Polyunsaturated Fat (grams)	Cholesterol (milligrams)
OILS						
Canola (rapeseed) (1 tbsp.)	120	14	*	8	4	0
Coconut (1 tbsp.)	120	14	12	*	*	0
Corn (1 tbsp.)	120	14	2	3	8	0
Cottonseed (1 tbsp.)	120	14	4	2	7	0
Grapeseed (1 tbsp.)	120	14	1	2	10	0
Olive (1 tbsp.)	120	14	2	10	1	0
Palm (1 tbsp.)	120	14	7	5	1	0
Palm kernel (1 tbsp.)	120	14	11	2	*	0
Peanut (1 tbsp.)	120	14	2	6	4	0
Safflower (1 tbsp.)	120	14	1	2	10	0
Sesame (1 tbsp.)	120	14	2	5	6	0
Soybean (1 tbsp.)	120	14	2	6	5	0
Sunflower (1 tbsp.)	120	14	1	3	9	0
Walnut (1 tbsp.)	120	14	1	3	9	0

Food/Portion	Calories	Total Fat (grams)	Saturated Fat (grams)	Protein (grams)	Carbohydrates (grams)	Cholesterol (milligrams)
BREADS, PASTA, GRAINS, LEGUMES, NUTS						
Bread, rye (1 oz.)	69	*	*	3	15	*
Bread, white, enriched (1 oz.)	57	*	*	2	14	*
Bread, whole wheat (1 oz.)	69	1	*	3	13	*
Crackers, graham (4 squares)	109	3	*	2	21	0
Crackers, saltine (10)	123	3	*	3	20	0
Doughnut, raised, glazed (1)	170	10	2	2	19	11
English muffin (1)	130	1	*	4	26	n/a
Roll, frankfurter or hamburger (1)	119	2	*	3	21	2
Roll, hard (1)	156	2	*	5	30	2
Tortilla, corn (1)	67	1	*	2	3	0
Macaroni, cooked (½ cup)	99	*	*	3	20	0
Noodles, egg, cooked (½ cup)	106	1	*	4	20	26
Rice, brown, cooked (½ cup)	108	*	*	3	22	0
Rice, white, enriched, cooked (½ cup)	132	*	*	3	29	0
Beans, black, dried, cooked (½ cup)	114	*	*	8	20	0
Beans, pinto, dried, cooked (½ cup)	117	*	*	7	22	0
Lentils, dried, cooked (½ cup)	115	*	*	9	20	0
Soybeans, dried, cooked (½ cup)	149	8	1	14	9	0
Almonds, whole, shelled (1 oz.)	167	15	1	6	6	0
Cashews, salted, roasted in oil (1 oz.)	163	14	3	5	8	0
Peanuts, salted, roasted in oil (1 oz.)	165	14	2	7	5	0
Peanut butter (1 tbsp.)	95	8	1	5	3	0
Pecans, halves (1 oz.)	189	19	2	2	5	0
Walnuts, English, pieces (1 oz.)	182	18	2	4	5	0
OTHER FATS, EGGS, DAIRY						
Butter (1 tbsp.)	102	12	7	*	*	31
Lard (1 tbsp.)	116	13	5	*	*	12
Margarine, corn oil, hard (stick) (1 tbsp.)	102	11	2	*	*	0
Margarine, safflower, soft (tub) (1 tbsp.)	101	11	1	0	0	0
Mayonnaise, whole-egg (1 tbsp.)	99	11	2	*	*	8
Vegetable shortening, hydrogenated (1 tbsp.)	113	13	3	0	0	0
Egg, whole, raw (1 large)	75	5	2	6	*	213

* Contains less than 1 gram

Food/Portion	Calories	Total Fat (grams)	Saturated Fat (grams)	Protein (grams)	Carbohydrates (grams)	Cholesterol (milligrams)
OTHER FATS, EGGS, DAIRY (continued)						
Egg yolk, raw (1)	59	5	2	3	*	213
Egg white, raw (1)	17	0	0	4	*	0
Buttermilk, cultured (1 cup)	98	2	1	8	12	10
Condensed milk, sweetened, canned (¼ cup)	246	7	4	6	42	26
Evaporated milk, skim, canned (¼ cup)	50	*	*	5	7	3
Evaporated milk, whole, canned (¼ cup)	84	5	3	4	6	18
Milk, whole (1 cup)	149	8	5	8	11	34
Milk, lowfat, 2% (1 cup)	122	5	3	8	12	20
Milk, skim or nonfat (1 cup)	86	*	*	8	12	5
Milk, whole, chocolate (1 cup)	208	8	5	8	26	30
Creamer, nondairy, liquid (1 tbsp.)	20	2	*	*	2	0
Creamer, nondairy, powder (2 tbsp.)	64	4	4	*	6	0
Half-and-half (1 tbsp.)	20	2	1	*	*	6
Sour cream (1 tbsp.)	31	3	2	*	*	6
Sour cream, reduced-fat (1 tbsp.)	25	2	1	1	1	5
Whipping cream (1 tbsp.)	43	5	3	*	*	17
Whipped cream, pressurized (1 tbsp.)	10	*	*	*	*	3
Dessert topping, nondairy (1 tbsp.)	9	*	*	*	*	*
Yogurt, whole, plain (8 oz.)	138	7	5	8	11	29
Yogurt, lowfat, plain (8 oz.)	143	4	2	12	16	14
Yogurt, lowfat, fruit-flavored (8 oz.)	231	2	2	10	43	9
Yogurt, nonfat, plain (8 oz.)	127	*	*	13	17	5
Cheese						
American (1 oz.)	106	9	6	6	*	27
Blue (1 oz.)	100	8	5	6	*	21
Brie (1 oz.)	95	8	n/a	6	*	28
Cheddar (1 oz.)	114	9	6	7	*	30
Cheese spread, process, American (1 oz.)	87	6	4	5	2	16
Cottage cheese, creamed (½ cup)	108	5	3	13	3	16
Cottage cheese, dry curd (½ cup)	62	*	*	13	1	5
Cottage cheese, lowfat, 2% fat (½ cup)	102	2	1	16	4	9
Cream cheese (1 oz.)	99	10	6	2	*	31
Gouda (1 oz.)	101	8	5	7	*	32
Gruyère (1 oz.)	117	9	5	8	*	31
Jack (1 oz.)	106	9	n/a	7	*	25
Mozzarella, whole milk (1 oz.)	80	6	4	6	*	22
Mozzarella, part skim (1 oz.)	72	5	3	7	*	16
Neufchâtel (1 oz.)	74	7	4	3	*	22
Parmesan (1 oz.)	129	9	5	12	1	22
Ricotta, whole milk (½ cup)	214	16	10	14	4	63
Ricotta, part skim (½ cup)	170	10	6	14	6	38
Roquefort (1 oz.)	105	9	5	6	*	26
Swiss (1 oz.)	107	8	5	8	*	26
Frozen Desserts						
Frozen yogurt, lowfat (½ cup)	113	1	n/a	3	23	4
Frozen yogurt, nonfat (½ cup)	110	0	0	2	24	0
Ice cream, rich, 16% fat (½ cup)	175	12	7	2	16	44
Ice cream, regular, 10% fat (½ cup)	134	7	4	2	16	30
Ice milk, regular (½ cup)	92	3	2	3	14	9
Ice milk, soft serve (½ cup)	112	2	1	4	19	7
Sherbet, orange (½ cup)	135	2	1	1	39	7

* Contains less than 1 gram

Index